BrandsFormation™

BrandsFormation™

HOW TO TRANSFORM
A GOOD SMALL BUSINESS
INTO A GREAT LOCAL BRAND

Chuck Mefford

LIGHTHOUSE COMMUNICATIONS

ISBN 978-0-9815850-0-0

To my wife, Roann,
and my sons Matt, Jon, Luke and Levi.
You are my inspiration.
Thanks for your love, support and all the laughter!

Acknowledgments

TO THE "BUILDERS"

The process of compiling this book, for me, seemed much like the process of building a sailboat. You begin with a good design. Next, you gather the materials and the team you need to construct a finely-tuned sailing vessel. Then, piece by piece it is assembled ... a solid, well-crafted ship that will survive the roughest Great Lakes storm.

I am deeply indebted to the "builders" in my life. You are the gurus, leaders, teachers, mentors and friends that have shown me the way. You have helped to shape this book and my career, and to you I say, "Thanks Mate!"

In alphabetical order:
Dave and Joy Adams, Randy Allsbury, Joe Belli, Chuck Benfer, Bob Berdan, Brian Blackburn, Bob Bolak, Bob Bucholtz, Richard Bucknor, BJ Bueno, Jim Butler, Wayne Cornils, Dr. Terry Cowgill, Bill Curtis, Joe Daguanno, Rick D'Amico, Scott Dennison, Bruce Docker, David Doetsch, Kimberly Dzumba, Pat Ebertz, Phil Fisher, Robert C. Fisher, Howard Gloede, Goldie, Bob and Doris Hale, Don Hicks, Linn Hodgson, John Hunt, Kevan Kavanaugh, Tom Kozer, Tom Kushak, Al Leighton, Bob Leighton, Jeff Leighton, Doug Loy, Chris Lytle, Chris Maddock, Kelley McDonald, Sara McMurray, Charles D. Mefford, Gayle Mefford, Jenny Mefford, John Meyer, Monica Musich,

Jolene Neis, Denny Niess, Ken Oberdorff, Gayle Olson, Kathy Parker, Tan Parker, Men of Phi Alpha, Jonathon Rand, Dick Record, Eric Rhoads, Bill Rittman, Carl Rohman, Marty "McFly" Schibblehut, Jeffery Schmidt, Brad Schrock, Carl Smith, John Sowada, Mark "Spinny" Spinabella, Ron Steinman, Tim Stevenson, Don Stoeckly, Mel Suhr, The Three Stooges, Theresa "TK" Timm, Lori Tradup, Jack Trout, Rob Vanderbeck, Brandon Vincent, Ted Waldbillig, Bill Walker, Tom Walker, Karole White, Jim Williams, and Roy Williams.

There are so many people to whom I owe thanks that I am bound to leave out someone. If that someone is you, I am sorry. It is an oversight on my part, and I sincerely apologize.

Foreword

The information in this book can change your life. It changed mine. Did I just say that? That's the kind of talk you might expect to read in a self-help book, but not a book about branding your business.

A business is more than the services or products it provides. Most people will say that making a profit is really what it is all about, and in part, this is true. But from my point of view, there is so much more.

To the small business owner: What was it about owning a business that you just couldn't do without? Owning a business is often very difficult. It comes with working long hours, great responsibility, and untold risk. Why is it that you took that leap of faith when most people don't? I believe the main force that drives business owners is the "entrepreneurial spirit." It is the dreamer, the visionary, and the leader inside. It is that feeling that drives you to create a path rather than just follow one. It can be so powerful, that if you don't follow the dream, you feel a sense of uneasiness and unfulfilled purpose.

I understand the challenges of building a successful business. My name is Brandon Vincent. There was a time when I was working as hard as I could and yet my business was losing money. I was worried about my future. I was worried about the future of my employees. I had built relationships with them, and their livelihoods and families depended on me. It was beginning to look like I might join the thousands of other small business owners who had to close shop and return to work for someone else. This was a frustrating and often painful period in my life.

Yet, I couldn't give up, because the business was a success in so many ways. My employees did a great job, and our customer service was excellent. We just lacked one very important thing: We didn't have enough customers. There are so many other great businesses that are missing their financial goals because they don't have enough customers, either.

Advertising is generally considered the way to reach the most consumers, but there are so many ways to advertise these days. It's really hard to know what the most efficient use of your money is. I can tell you more than you'll ever want to know about residential or commercial painting ... but advertising? It's not an area that most of us have any real knowledge or training in, and that makes it feel even more risky.

To compound the problem, whom can you trust? With so many media sales reps selling everything from magnets to billboards, and swarming like bees to honey telling you their medium is the best, it can be maddening. Be careful — and I'm talking from experience here. Just because you spend a lot of money, and maybe even reach a lot of people with your advertising, it doesn't mean you are getting a good return on your investment.

Looking back over the years when my business was struggling, I tried everything I could to stop the bleeding. But I did it in all the wrong ways, and it really hurt my bottom line. Luckily for me I attended a seminar called BrandsFormation™ by Chuck Mefford, which, I said earlier, changed my life. Let me explain.

That day, I was taught the principles and techniques in this book. For the first time, strategy and advertising made sense to me. I understood how to get a return on my ad dollars; and more importantly, I now had a system for bringing in new customers.

Since that seminar, many good things have resulted from the changes I made. Our company hasn't changed much, in the sense that we still take good care of our employees and customers. Yet, the differences are crucial. We have had excellent sales growth, and this has helped my company become very profitable. What has this done for me personally? It has allowed me to work fewer hours, it has afforded my family financial stability, and it has helped make my business dream a reality.

I would like to share that I have been blessed to know Chuck on a personal level since attending his seminar years ago. One thing I really respect about Chuck is that his life is not driven by making money, but by making a positive difference. I believe that if you trust and work his system as I have, then you, too, can turn your great business into a great local brand.

Brandon Vincent
Genesis Painting
Madison, WI

Contents

Introduction

You may be the best at what you do. You may have a great story to tell. But if no one knows, what's the point? My goal for writing this book is to give you a proven system and the courage to brand your business for dramatic growth.

I've spent much of my life on what I'll call a "branding odyssey." There's not much I haven't witnessed. I have made my share of mistakes along the way, but every success and every failure has offered an invaluable lesson in what it takes to brand a business. One of the most important things I have discovered in my 30 years of marketing is: It's not a question of *"How good is your business?"* It's a question of *"How good is your marketing?"*

The road to success for any business is constantly changing. There is more competition in every category. No matter if you are a plumber or a plastic surgeon, you have increased competition. To compound the situation, it is difficult to reach preoccupied consumers who are distracted by thousands of messages coming at them everyday.

Instead of focusing on what you can't control – things such as expanding competition and the amount of messages blasted at consumers – my system helps you focus on the things you can control:

- You can be the business that people think of first when they want or need your product or service.

- You can own mental real estate in the minds of consumers.
- You can get a measurable return on your advertising investment.
- You can create an emotional connection with consumers.

BrandsFormation™ is an easy and doable system that can help anyone take their good small business and transform it into a great local brand.

I am not asking you to read this book and apply my system because I think it will work for you. I am asking you because I know that my system has worked for thousands of business owners. It can work for you, too.

1

The Power of BrandsFormation™

Let's face it: You can waste a lot of money in advertising! You may have already. Isn't it time to change the way you've been doing things? If you'll stick with me through this book, I'll show you how to get an incredible amount of leverage out of a modest marketing budget, and how you can gain significant mindshare and market share in your category, whatever your profession.

You are an enthusiastic, smart dental school grad ready to start your own practice! Your five-year plan includes putting yourself in debt by several hundred thousand dollars.

Your competition: You look at the business horizon and you see a community filled with established dentists. You are the new kid on the block.

Your challenge: How do you build up your practice? How will you set yourself apart from the competition?

* * *

You are a steady and honest owner of a tow-truck company. Who needs a tow-truck? Someone whose car has broken down. Who thinks about tow-truck companies any other time? No one.

Your competition: Large national companies are buying up towing and repair businesses, and have giant marketing budgets compared to yours. You're primarily a *Yellow Pages* guy. Now there are 20 other tow-truck ads next to yours. The *Yellow Pages* doesn't work like it used to, and now they've got three different books!

Your challenge: How can you get people to think of you first when they need a tow?

* * *

You are the owner of a good heating and air conditioning business. Your work ethic and commitment to the customer is a definite asset.

Your competition: You are one of many heating and air conditioning businesses all over town.

Your challenge: You have been in business for several years, and your "word of mouth" is good … it's just working very slowly. How can you get your name out quicker and be the guy people turn to when they need heating and air conditioning services?

* * *

These are real businesses and real situations. They are each well-run businesses trying to carve out their place among consumers and grow to the next level. You'll discover how each is a success today because they learned and applied the fundamentals of BrandsFormation™. Just as David took down Goliath with a stone and a sling, they used the four fundamentals of my system to slay their giants — the competition.

KNOW THE BATTLEFIELD

"All marketing battles take place in the mind," says Jack Trout, one of the founders and pioneers in positioning theory. "It's a mind game."[1]

That's why I speak of capturing mindshare, and "owning words" in the mind. To find out how you are doing, you only need to answer one question:

"When I mention your product or service to people in your area, what company or business do they think of first?"

You want them to think of you first. Capturing mindshare or owning mental real estate is what branding and BrandsFormation™ is all about. **Owning mental real estate — that's how the big guys got big!** If you want to compete with them, you've got to know how to play their game. BrandsFormation™ is your play guide. Upon completion of this book you will have a better understanding of why branding your business is crucial for your success. And, if you apply my principles just as many before you have done, you too will own mental real estate and transform your business.

3

THE OPPORTUNITY AND FREEDOM
OF SMALL BUSINESSES

I have a passion for small-business America. Though I've worked with some of the largest companies in America, my real drive comes from the desire to see small businesses succeed. The David versus Goliath thing always gets me. I believe in David. If you own or manage a good small business, I believe in you and this book is for you. Your good business can become a great local brand, in spite of that "big box" store or bigger local Goliath.

Big business often gets the glory, but small businesses built America. Small businesses put food on the table of families, provide jobs, and make communities better places to live. Some studies have indicated that small businesses contribute more than 70% to our economy.

Because of the incredible freedom, opportunity, and resources found in this nation, small businesses have always been the way talented, smart, and motivated individuals have carved out their unique stories of success. You may have heard of "The Small Business Owner's Creed": "Professionals built the Titanic; amateurs built the Ark." Even with all the challenges of this rapidly changing world, small businesses still provide the most fertile ground around for ambitious men and women to go for it — to pursue their dreams, exercise their personal autonomy, and unleash their creative talents — without being hamstrung by the bureaucracies, red tape, and glacial pace of large corporations.

My father, along with his partners, bought a small business for $184,000. He sold it 24 years later for $11 million — which leads me to one last point: If you do this right, you can get "filthy, stinking rich"! However, to me, sales, profits, or cash flow are just measures of how well you run your business, not necessarily "the goal."

Jack Trout has changed the business world through his visionary and critical work, bringing clear concepts of strategy and positioning to the largest corporations, including Papa John's and Southwest Airlines. But he told me a little secret: the small business owner really has an advantage. He pointed out that, precisely because they don't have to deal with Wall Street, large organizations, or complicated boards, small business owners can stop, turn on a dime, learn and implement effective principles of branding. And he affirmed that many of the principles of strategy he taught to the largest companies in the world are exactly the same as those that can be applied by a sole proprietor.

SAFETY AND SUCCESS THROUGH PRACTICING PROVEN PRINCIPLES

Besides building a winning strategy and accelerating the growth of small businesses, my other passion is sailing. Like the business world, sailing attracts people who clearly know what they are doing and people who clearly don't. There are many foolish people who venture into Lake Michigan thinking, "What could be so hard about sailing? You just hoist the sail, point the boat in the right direction and hold her steady." These are the ones who think there's no real danger on anything called a "lake." They think recommended check-lists and procedures are for those who lack self-confidence. And these are the ones, like an acquaintance of mine, who tear out the bottom of their sailboats by running them upon unseen rocks.

If you care about life and property and you want to get the best out of your boat, you will learn and abide by the proven principles of seamanship. You will learn and practice the check-lists and procedures, because you know they are important. You will accept that there are fixed points that won't adjust their reality for anyone, like lighthouses and rocks. And you will learn and apply the principles for responding to changing conditions on the water, because you know that you live in an unpredictable world. A calm and serene lake can turn into raging, six-foot white caps in a matter of minutes. These principles of sailing and navigation are very similar to the principles of running a successful business. I will share with you the fixed, unchanging principles and universal laws of nature and business you will have to reckon with, plus strategies you can use to avoid a few storms and navigate your way effectively through an unpredictable, changing business environment.

YOU CAN GET THERE!

I have emails documenting wonderful success stories, a few of which I'll share with you along the way. You'll be inspired and encouraged as you read how business owners like you applied these concepts and dramatically "brandsformed" their businesses. Many were owners of good small businesses, but were mainly discouraged when it came to effective marketing that showed any kind of ROI (return on investment).

Most business owners don't know how to get ROI out of their ad dollars. The majority aren't sure what works, but I do hear once in a while, "Word of mouth is best!" The simple truth is, if you have a "good" business and good word of mouth, you can grow it, albeit slowly. With BrandsFormation™ you can grow it much faster — it's accelerated word of mouth. It starts with asking the right questions. Think these over and keep them in mind as we proceed:

- **Who** are you and **why** should I do business with you?
  *This is your **"elevator speech."** You have 15 seconds to answer.*

- Can you fill in the blank?
  *People do not buy products or services. **People buy what products or services** _____ .*

- Is there a **single word, set of words, or phrase** I can say to someone, and that person will tell me the name of your business?

- Do you know how the **human mind** works, and how it affects your strategy to gain **"mental real estate"** and grow sales?

- Do you know how to take advantage of iconic and echoic memory?

- Do you know the **three biggest blunders** companies make in advertising, and how to avoid them?

- Do you have a system to **evaluate the effectiveness** of your advertising dollars?

- How has the business landscape changed during the last three years in your category?

- What have you done to become a "top of mind" product or service?

- Do competitors own mindshare? Do they own "a word" or "a phrase"?

BrandsFormation™ has worked for small businesses across the country. It can work for you, too! I hope you'll later take the time to share the results with me, because I love to hear all of your success stories! You can see many successful business owners right now at my website: **www.lighthousecommunications.us**. Click on Video and enjoy!

Breaking it Down

CHAPTER 1

When I mention your product or service to people in your area, what company or business do they think of first?

- You want people to think of you first. You want to own mental real estate. Remember, mindshare = market share.

- A great strategy and a well-written message can help compensate for a limited advertising budget.

- Small business owners have an advantage. They have the ability to stop, turn on a dime, and learn and implement effective principles to successfully brand themselves.

- If your business has *good word of mouth*, BrandsFormation™ will accelerate it more quickly and more dramatically.

www.brandsformation.com

2

Give Me a Reason to Do Business with You

Let me present my opening question a better way:

"Who are you, and why should I do business with you?"

This is your chance to give your "elevator speech." You have 15 seconds to give it before you lose my attention or the doors open. No rambling, mumbling, beating around the bush, or stuttering. No time to think. You should know the answer RIGHT NOW, and deliver it in a memorable and vivid way.

Most importantly, you have to tell me what I really want to know. Do you know what that is?

People do not buy products or services. **People buy what products or services** _____.

If you don't know the answer, then learning and applying this single truth will itself justify the price of this book!

ANYONE CAN HAVE A "GOOD" BUSINESS, BUT YOU NEED A GREAT STRATEGY TO HAVE A GREAT BUSINESS

If you've been around long enough, you hear everything. It's no wonder business owners can't get a solid handle on what's right and what direction to take. I've had more than 30 years in business, flown more than two million airline miles, and worked with countless business owners across America. I have had a front row seat to witness first hand why some businesses succeed and others fail.

How good businesses become great businesses is more than luck, more than the best training, more than the best people and best company policies. To be sure, those are important, but even all together, they won't help you reach your destination.

For great businesses, it's all about great strategy, and this book will help you build one. But it's impossible to have a great strategy without first understanding a few things about you and your business category.

WHY DO PEOPLE BUY?

People do not buy products or services.
People buy what products or services _DO FOR THEM!_
Ask yourself these questions. Would you rather buy:

- A *mattress?* Or, a *good night's sleep?*
- A *Harley?* Or, *freedom on the open road?*
- *Clothing?* Or, *"A Look"?*
- An *RV?* Or, *family fun?*

Once it's asked, you know the right answers, don't you? People always buy the **benefit** that comes from a product or service.

Start thinking about *your* product or service. What does your product or service actually *DO* for your customers or patients?

THE BENEFIT IS THE HOOK

I not only teach these principles; like everyone else, I'm subject to them.

As I mentioned earlier, I love sailing. My first sailing experiences happened as a young Boy Scout and with my dad on small Wisconsin and Michigan lakes. For years I had resisted the call of the beautiful lakes and shorelines, and fought the urge to buy a sailboat. That all changed one day when I was talking to a good friend (and soon-to-be sailboat partner). He asked me a great question: "*Why* do you want to buy a sailboat?"

Boat salesmen had always talked about this boat or that boat, this diesel engine, or that sail — but none had ever asked me *why* I wanted to buy my own boat. I immediately started mumbling about my sons and my wife, dreaming about the wonderful summers we could enjoy sailing and exploring the Great Lakes together as a family.

I realized that until now whenever I was shopping for a sailboat, sales presentations about "the design," "this keel," or "that sail" did nothing for me. But my soon-to-be sailboat partner didn't talk about a boat. He told me things a sailboat *could do for me*. He had nautical charts showing northern Lake Michigan, not far from where I lived. He

13

pointed out Mackinac Island, Beaver Island, Gold Coast, North Channel. "You can be like pirates with your boys," he said, "and your wife will love shopping in the charming little towns. Think of all the great family fun times ahead."

My partner needed a partner, and he was smart. He didn't sell me "boat ownership." He helped me envision the fun times I would have visiting different islands, and sailing with my family — just spending time and loving life together. You see, my soon-to-be partner was selling (and I was buying) *family fun and great memories.* The sailboat was just a means to those ends. I got a great family lifestyle, and my friend got himself a partner. It was a "win-win" for all.

The same thing happened when Roann, my wife, decided to do some remodeling. She has an unerring nose for high quality things (what I call "expensive stuff"). We were redoing the entryway of our home, and a salesman was showing her samples of floor covering. Like a homing pigeon, Roann's eye quickly picked out the "highest quality" wood samples.

Do you know what that salesman *didn't* say? "Let me tell you about the 10-year warranty." He *didn't* explain all the features and details.

He just said, "Mrs. Mefford, imagine your friends, neighbors, and family coming into this entryway, and going, 'WOW!'"

I knew, right then, it was all over. Who can compete with "WOW!"? That salesman went right for the jugular. She wasn't buying floor materials; she was buying the "WOW!" It had nothing to do with the floor, and everything to do with what that floor *did for her.*

(So if you ever pop in for a visit, don't forget to look

down when you walk in and respond appropriately. I will thank you!)

WHAT ARE *YOU* TALKING ABOUT?

Look at some of your current or past advertising. Are you talking about the same products and services everyone else has? **Or are you talking about what your product or services** *do for your customers?* Be honest!

Someone sent me a great commercial they ran across on YouTube. It goes something like this:

A young 20-something man is walking through a grocery store produce department with a five-year-old child. The little boy says he wants some candy and the father says, "No." At this point the child erupts, shouting, "I want a sweetie! I want a sweetie!" Other shoppers stop and look. The kid starts running around, screaming, and knocking over displays and throwing products onto the floor.

Passersby glare at the man. He stares vacantly into space, communicating helplessness.

The child screams continuously while he wreaks havoc. He falls to the floor, punching, kicking, and screaming at the top of his lungs.

Cut back to the young man. His face is expressionless and hopeless.

What in the world is the product? What could this commercial be advertising? Audiences have no idea what's coming. Two simple words appear on the screen:

USE CONDOMS

It's an unexpected turn. But the manufacturer, Zazoo Condoms, has hit a home run. They have cut right to the chase. It tells what the product does for you, without even referring to the product until the very end.

If you take away nothing else from this book, get this down: People do not buy products or services. They buy what products and services *do for them*. That's what you want to talk about in your marketing and ads!

A GREAT LOCAL BUSINESS DOES NOT EQUAL A GREAT LOCAL BRAND

Scott Bedbury is the marketing guru behind the highly successful Starbucks and Nike branding campaigns. This is a guy who knows a thing or two about branding. After a personal shopping experience, he once remarked,

> **I walked through a hardware store last night, and I came across fifty brands I didn't know existed. They may be great products, but they're not great brands.**[2]

There *is* a huge difference!

Finding a good business is not difficult. Maybe yours fits in that category. *But being a good business is not the same thing as being a "great" local brand.*

What makes a great brand? If someone needs whatever it is you're selling, *does that person think of you first, and have some kind of logical or emotional connection with you?*

That is the essence of branding. That's what you're after. The great thing about it: *You* can apply the very same principles as those employed by the "big guys." The *BrandsFormation*™ System shows you the way.

For now, concentrate on step one, your elevator speech. Get to work and come up with your succinct and benefit-focused answer to the question with which I began this chapter: "Who are you, and why should I do business with you?"

And by now, you know what I'm *really* asking you:

"What will your product or service _DO FOR ME_?"

When you have your answer, you're ready to move to the next step.

Breaking it Down

CHAPTER 2

- A great business does not equal a great brand.

- Go to work on your elevator speech.

- Don't talk about the same old stuff that everyone else is.

- People don't buy products or services, they buy what that product or service does for them. What does your product or service really do for the customer?

- Come up with a short, benefit-focused answer to the question, *"Who are you and why should I do business with you?"* What am I really asking? **What will your product or service do for me?**

www.brandsformation.com

Even if you do <u>nothing</u>, change happens every day!

3

Mega Changes
and Mega Choices!

You absolutely must have a sharply-focused, benefit-based — *what's in it for me?* — message to begin. After that, you can begin to find a way to communicate it through the noise of daily life.

Even if you have a perfectly-honed message, you still have the problem of how to be heard in the world, a world that has changed dramatically during the past few decades. An overwhelming number of voices are screaming every day, "Buy me!"

YOUR CHOICE: CHAINS OR CHANGE?

Constant and rapid change has become the norm. You must understand how to navigate the world you are now living and working in. You will either be chained to the past, with its out-of-date and ineffective thinking and practices, or you will embrace the changes that have come about in the last 40 years, and especially the last decade.

I did a Google search of the three words: business books change. There were 23,300,000 results! Change is the topic of speculation in countless articles and bestselling business books. We are living today in a tidal wave of rapid change.

Even if we do *nothing*, change happens every day. If you have a white fence post and do nothing, what will you eventually have? You will end up with a dirty, rotting fence post.

If you have a nice grass lawn and do nothing, what will you eventually have? A yard full of weeds.

If you do nothing in the way of exercise or dietary discipline, what kind of body will you eventually have? It's not pretty, so let's not go there, please!

Don't waste your breath griping about how you hate change. Change is unavoidable. What matters is your response. It's simply a matter of choice — even if you choose to do nothing, that's a choice! You can choose to adapt and exploit change, or you can be chained to the past, do nothing and fade into obscurity.

"MADE IN JAPAN"

What does that phrase say to you? I remember when growing up in the 1960s and '70s, "Made in Japan" meant cheap or flimsy. Today, those same words, "Made in Japan," mean quality and reliability. Think Toyota, Lexus, and Sony. That's what I call *change*!

You can't evade it. We've become a MySpace, YouTube, Facebook world. A growing percentage of consumer activities are being transacted online — everything from cars, to clothes, to homes. Every year, online holiday shopping breaks all previous records. Many restaurant orders are now made online instead of by phone. Soon, that will be surpassed by orders made through text-messaging.

You are better off learning to love and manage change to your benefit. Okay, "loving" change may be too much to ask, but **responding to change effectively is crucial to remaining competitive!**

HARSH CHANGING REALITY

Let's talk more change. Let's talk Hewlett Packard. One of their goals is to make some of their products obsolete 18 months after their market introduction. Why would they do that? "They want to sell more stuff," right? Well, yes, they do, but it's more strategic than that. What they are really saying is, "If we don't continue working on the cutting edge, if we don't keep reinventing ourselves, if we don't keep rolling out new products, if we don't keep changing — *our competition will.*"

Gillette is a master at managing change. They still have a 60% market share today, which is phenomenal for a company that had that same kind of market share 30-40 years ago. In contrast, General Motors and Ford were the dominant automakers in the 1960s; today they are behind Toyota worldwide.

How does Gillette maintain that market share year after year? Every year they roll out new products. They recently introduced a razor with three blades and a battery in the handle! It makes you wonder how many blades we'll eventually get in a single razor. Maybe it'll end up being like a Swiss army razor with laser beam technology and MP3. Then we can sing while we shave.

Crazy? Maybe. But Gillette knows that if they don't do it, *their competitors will.* That's how they stay on top. They keep reinventing themselves.

These companies have learned to manage change based on customer needs. So can you.

Wal-Mart is another big player determined to make change work for them as well as their customers. In the wise words of Sam Walton, "You can't just keep doing what works one time. Everything around you is always changing. To succeed, stay out in front of that change." Wal-Mart has created, Wal-Mart "Out in Front," a focus in five areas where they are committed to staying "out in front."

VISIT THE GRAVEYARD

Still hesitant? Think you can ignore reality? I've got two words for you: Wards and Olds.

1. *Wards.* Last holiday season, how much of your shopping was done at Montgomery Ward? Why do I bring up Wards? Because people shopped there for more than 125 years! What happened? The company that innovated the "satisfaction guaranteed or your money back" policy, which was so popular among consumers for years, closed its doors in 2001. No one knew what Wards was anymore. They lost their identity. They lost their brand.

2. ***Oldsmobile.*** This is a crying shame. The oldest
   automobile brand in America. Founded in 1897 —
   Defunct in 2004! What happened? By the 1990s,
   the brand had lost its place in the market, and they
   struggled from that point forward. They looked
   like any of 600 different makes and models
   on the road. No one knew what an Olds was
   anymore. They lost their identity. They lost their
   brand.

That tells you that even huge companies with massive
executive and marketing budgets can forget the
fundamentals and lose their way. That confirms that size
is not the answer, for them or for you. It is always about
the fundamentals of strategy and how people think.

Wards and Olds lost their brand. They looked and
sounded like everyone else. There was nothing in our
minds anymore that made them "better" or "different."

CHANGING TIMES FOR YOUR INDIVIDUAL CUSTOMER OR CLIENT

It's not just *change.* We live in an era of mega choices.
The number of competitors has exploded exponentially
in every category, whether you are a door company or a
dentist.

The following chart gives a snapshot of the number of
choices available to consumers in the early 1970s
compared to those available less than three decades later.

These are just a few categories, but they show clearly
why people experience decision-paralysis. **Consumers are**

overwhelmed with product choices in just about every category. Imagine what the updated figures will show at the end of this decade, or the next!

The Explosion of Choices[3]		
Category	Choices in early 1970s	Choices in late 1990s
McDonald's Menu	13	43
Breakfast Cereals	160	340
Pop-Tarts	3	29
Frito-Lay Chips	10	79
Dental Floss	12	64
Mouthwashes	15	66
Running Shoes	5	85
Pain Relievers	17	141

Take just two examples. When I was a kid, one of the most prominent breakfast cereals was *Cheerios*. Have you been to the grocery store lately? There are at least eight more flavors of *Cheerios* to choose from, including *Apple Cinnamon, Yogurt Burst, Honey Nut, MultiGrain, Frosted, Berry Burst, Fruity Cheerios*, and *Cheerios Crunch*. The same thing has happened to another American classic, *Oreo* cookies. Last I counted, Nabisco is making more than 30 options for us, not counting the special holiday versions. Your children or grandchildren are growing up in a different world.

Besides all the options, **consumers are bombarded with advertising messages every day**, many of them backed by the huge advertising resources of the big guys, like General Motors, McDonald's, or Procter & Gamble.

How are you going to carve out your place? How will you break through? It's no wonder consumers have developed ways and means of tuning out advertising. That's why Bond and Kirschenbaum, authors of *Under the Radar: Talking to Today's Cynical Consumer* (1997), wrote, "Most ads wind up in our 'mental garbage pail,' discarded like yesterday's half-eaten tuna sandwich."[4]

Just how many more businesses are there in your category that weren't there 30, 10, or five years ago? There are more insurance agents, more pharmacies, more dentists, more lawyers, and on and on.

Now, you also have competition from category killers. Sounds bad, doesn't it? Well, it can be if you're not prepared. What is the risk to the little local stationery and office supply store when Office Depot comes to town?

Take Home Depot. It's not really one store. It's more like 57 stores, all under one roof. If you do driveways, you're up against Home Depot. Do you do kitchens? Home Depot is your competitor. Do you sell appliances? For the past several years, Home Depot has been taking market share from Sears, who held the top spot in appliances for years. Do you repair roofs? Fencing? Guess who's your Goliath?

WORRIED?

The "big guys" are not the "bad guys." I do not tell you these things to discourage you. I'm simply stating a business reality.

Did you see the 1994 hit, *Dumb and Dumber?* There is a scene in which Jim Carrey's character asks a gorgeous young woman about his chances to date her. "Are my chances 100 to 1?" No. "Are they 1,000 to 1?" No. "Are they one million to 1?" Yeah, that's about right.

"THEN YOU'RE SAYING I'VE GOT A CHANCE!"

It certainly appeared to be an uphill battle, but his response shows he wasn't about to give up. That same tenacious, believing attitude is what got you where you are today. And, that same tenacity and desire are crucial to develop your brand, and to the ultimate success of your brand. BrandsFormation™ is the system, and determination is the stance that will help you take down your Goliath!

> **Life's journey is not to arrive at the grave safely in a well-preserved body, but rather to skid in sideways, totally worn out, shouting, "Holy cow! What a ride!"**
>
> — *Unknown*

This quote typifies the attitude I see in successful small business owners. You've built a great business, now don't stop until you've transformed it into a great brand.

Breaking it Down

CHAPTER 3

- Change happens everyday, even if you do nothing!

- Are you chained to the past, or will you learn to make change work for your business?

- Manage change based on customer needs. If you don't, your competitors will.

- Responding to change effectively is crucial to remaining competitive.

- Today, there are more businesses and products in every category. You have more competition than ever before!

- Customers are overwhelmed with the explosion of product choices in every category.

- Potential customers are trying to find you in a sea of choices. How will you stand out? How will they find you?

www.brandsformation.com

4

Measuring Success in Advertising

I have two questions for you.

Before you answer: You must be realistic. Okay, Scout's honor …

First: How much money do you spend on advertising each year?

Second: Are you getting a good return on investment (ROI) with your ad dollars?

I think I already know the answer, because I've asked those same questions thousands of times to small business owners, and heard their loud and nearly unanimous response … we're frustrated!

Most have no idea whether or not there is any return on their ad budget, or how they might measure it in the first place. "Frankly," they say, "I'd rather keep it in my pocket and call it cash flow or profit, and go on a vacation."

For small business owners, advertising means a huge gamble, a shot in the dark, a blindfolded dart throw, or, worst of all, pouring money down a black hole of "see you later, Sucker."

IT DOESN'T HAVE TO BE THAT WAY!

Advertising *can* be measured. Unfortunately, most business owners take what I call the "Baskin-Robbins approach to advertising strategy: 31 flavors; you pick." Their "marketing plan" is based on which salesman most recently walked in the door with the latest idea, and they picked that "flavor," at least for that month. It's a reactive approach and it rarely works.

Here's a revolutionary idea — now stay with me — instead of being reactive, build a proactive media plan with a measurable ROI. You probably have a payroll system. You may have a training system. You have a maintenance system. Then why not have a marketing system? Just take a "systems" approach to advertising.

BrandsFormation™ is a system that helps you leverage your limited advertising dollars to great results: owning mental real estate. No matter who your competitors are, you can become the business someone thinks of first whenever they want or need your product or service.

What do you need to start? Have you ever gone to a mall and wanted to find a particular store? You go to the display that shows a layout of the mall and where individual stores are located. There on the map you see the store you need. But guess what? You have to know one more bit of information: You have to know where you are now. That's why there's a little arrow with the caption, "You are here."

The same is true with your strategic advertising plans. Before you can decide where you want to go, you have to figure out where you are today. Let's begin with taking your three-year Ad Budget Test — your "You are here."

YOUR PRESENT REALITY

1. Write down how much money you've spent in the past year trying to reach people in your area. That includes television, radio, *Yellow Pages*, yearbooks, magnets — anything. Add up the figures. You don't have to show it to anyone. This is just for you. Be honest. That's the only way to get anywhere.

2. Multiply it by 3 (for years).

That's your three-year Present Reality. That's your starting point for comparison as you begin your BrandsFormation™.

Okay, you've spent that much trying to connect with people in your area to "come on in." How did it work? What do you have to show for your expenditures? What mental real estate do you own? If you've got that "shined deer look," then you've fallen into Advertising Blunder #1:

Advertising Blunder #1:
Spending advertising dollars without knowing how you will measure the return on investment (ROI).

I have a golden rule. Please adopt it for yourself.

Golden Rule for Advertising

Never spend a cent on any advertising until you first know how you are going to measure the ROI

Because of violating this rule, most small business operators are frustrated with their expenditures in advertising. Yet there are people who've spent money and are very happy. The difference, you ask? They have leveraged their dollars to brand their company into the minds of consumers effectively; they own mental real estate in people's heads. They have something to show for their money.

How can you measure whether or not you have captured mindshare? There are two ways. One, your annual profit and loss statement. Look for "annual sales." Second, you can hire a research company to discover where you appear in a "top of mind" survey. This will give you a baseline against which to measure future performance. The key here is "measurable." That's what you must identify first. "Of this hard-earned money I'm about to spend in advertising, how will I measure its effectiveness?"

WHAT EFFECTIVE BRANDING LOOKS LIKE

I bet I could go anywhere in your town, talk to people of almost any age, and ask them to finish this phrase: "You're in good hands with _____."

Most people would immediately say "Allstate."

They've been incredibly consistent, so much so that you wouldn't expect it any other way. Allstate's consistency has paid off handsomely. They own mental real estate.

How about some more phrases? Cover the right hand column and see how many companies you can name.

"Like a good neighbor, _____ is there."	*State Farm Insurance*
"Mmm, mmm, good!"	*Campbell's Soup*
"Fifteen minutes can save you 15% or more on your car insurance."	*Geico*
"Melts in your mouth, not in your hands."	*M&Ms*
"Gets the red out."	*Visine*
"Breakfast of champions."	*Wheaties*
"Good to the last drop."	*Maxwell House*
"Please Don't Squeeze the _____"	*Charmin Bathroom Tissue*
"The San Francisco Treat"	*Rice-a-Roni*
"Oh, I wish I were an _____"	*Oscar Meyer Wieners*

These companies have something you probably don't have. They own mental real estate. They can show ROI for their advertising investments.

"See the USA in your _____."

Baby boomers know it's "Chevrolet." The next example shows what branding staying power is all about, as well as illustrating the generation gap. Fill in the blank:

"Winston tastes good, _____."

I love asking this in my seminars. Many hands go up in recognition, while the rest of the audience is mystified. You can be sure that all the people raising their hands and replying "like a cigarette should" have grey hair — if they're fortunate enough to still have hair. Do you know why? Because the government outlawed all broadcast advertising of cigarettes in *1970*. That ad hasn't been heard over the airwaves in almost *40 years*, yet it's still branded in many people's minds!

WORDLESS BRANDING

You don't even have to use words. Pictures, colors, and sounds can become so associated with a product or service that people recognize it instantly.

If I show you a picture of golden arches, you think "McDonald's" in a nanosecond.

If I show you a picture of a man in a Kentucky gentleman's white suit, with white hair, moustache, and goatee, and ask you what slogan goes with it, you'll say, "Finger lickin' good!" That man's picture used to be labeled "Colonel Sanders" from *Kentucky Fried Chicken*. No name is necessary today. They've worked it so that all you need is the initials. They're simply *KFC*.

One company "owns a color": "What can Brown do for you?" UPS owns the color, brown. It's simple and easy, and it's a great example of strategy.

Do you know that one company has branded itself by using a sound? It includes just five notes — one long tone, followed by four short ones in a rising musical phrase. To show you how powerful this is, consider that almost no one has seen the product or even knows what the product is. "Intel inside." We just know we "have to have it" in our computer!

IT WORKS LOCALLY, TOO!

Here's the really cool part! You don't have to be a huge company to own mental real estate and get advertising ROI. Many local businesses own mental real estate in their towns. Here are a few examples from businesses my firm has worked with.

"Cowgill Dental keeps you smiling ... "
Dr. Terry Cowgill, DDS

"Pick your party at the ... "
Party Girls at the Party Tree

"More Madison homeowners trust us over anyone else! We color your world."
Brandon Vincent — Genesis Painting

"I want to be your Mortgage Man ... "
John Meyer — State Street Mortgage

"Two good ole, hard working, Wisconsin boys."
Mad City Roofing, Siding & Windows

These local small businesses own mental real estate, just like the big national companies. What do you own?

IT'S YOUR TURN

You might be a good small business, but your challenge is exactly the same. You must answer the question, just as these local business owners did:

> *"What word, slogan, or statement can I say, and have people tell me the name of your business?"*

Answering this question starts you on the path to determining your advertising ROI. After your last three years of advertising expenditures:
- Where are you in the market? Are you getting into people's heads?
- Do you own mental real estate, some word(s) or slogan?
- Are you branded into the minds of people with pictures, color, or sound?
- Have your sales increased (the ultimate measure)?
If your answers are not to your satisfaction, read on.

OTHERS HAVE DONE IT

Go to Madison, Wisconsin, and ask people on the street, "What's your favorite color?" A very high percentage won't say blue, red, or green. They'll answer, "Genesis Painting" — now the #1 residential painter in Madison. That's capturing mindshare.

If you're ever in Springfield, Illinois, ask, "Who makes it easy?" Three out of five people will reply, "Fritz Pfitzer." Fritz is just a single Realtor, but he has branded himself in the minds of consumers with one word. "Easy" (added to Fritz's blood, sweat, and tears, of course) has made Fritz consistently #1 or #2.

These businesses have captured mindshare. They are getting a return on their investment. Branding is working for them! It can work for you, too.

First, you want to avoid the other two biggest advertising blunders. That's what we'll examine in the next chapter.

Breaking it Down

- How much money do you spend (all types) in advertising? Are you happy with your return on investment (ROI)?

- **Avoid Advertising Blunder #1:** Spending advertising dollars without knowing how you will measure the return on investment (ROI).

- Take an honest look at your advertising expenditures for the past year and multiply it by 3 (years). This is your starting point, your basis for comparison as you begin your BrandsFormation™.

- ROI can be measured first by looking at annual sales. Second, you can hire a research firm to discover where you appear in a top-of-mind survey.

- Another way to determine ROI is *ownership* of a phrase, a word, a color or sound in the minds of consumers.

- Money well-spent will buy you mental real estate in the minds of consumers.

www.brandsformation.com

5

The Other Two Biggest Advertising Blunders

Small business owners spend and waste enormous amounts of money in advertising. That's because they tend to make some basic advertising blunders. Learn to avoid them, and you'll be way ahead of the game.

We've already discussed **Advertising Blunder #1: Spending advertising dollars without knowing how you will measure ROI.** Now let's talk about the second and third common blunders.

Advertising Blunder #2:
Media Mix-Up

Analogizing from my friend Jim Doyle, imagine in your hand an averaged-sized pitcher, three-quarters full of water.

This represents your total advertising budget.

"That's not enough," you might say. "I spend a lot of money on advertising."

I'm not sure what "a lot of money" means to you, but let me put it into perspective.

1. Sheer numbers of people.

Even if you're in a fairly small town, it would not be unusual for there to be 100,000–200,000 people within your geographical reach. Without a specific plan, you are trying to reach *all of them* using the cash you have available. If you tried to splash your pitcher of water on all of them, how wet would any individual get? There wouldn't be enough to baptize everyone by the sprinkling method.

2. Numbers and size of competitors.

There is a number batted around that today's consumer is hit with, on average, *5,000 advertising messages each day*. That means 4,999 other brands are also splashing away, pouring their pitchers into the consumers' minds.

Plus, many of these messages are coming from the national companies behind well-known brands like *Crest, Wheaties, Big Macs, Chevy* trucks, and *Tide*. And they've got 5,000 gallon drums to work with compared to your pitcher.

Still impressed with your advertising budget? Or are you feeling a little watered down?

LET'S TAKE A LOOK AT HOW MANY CUPS YOU ARE TRYING TO FILL

Here's where typical small business owners compound their mistakes, and dramatically reduce the impact of their advertising budgets.

Write on a piece of paper the various avenues you have used this year for advertising. By that I mean things like radio, television, *Yellow Pages*, direct mail, web page, print, door hangers — anything.

Now imagine that each medium you use is a cup. Two TV stations — that's two cups. Three stations — that's three cups. Here's the real question: How many cups are you trying to fill with your tiny pitcher of advertising dollars/water?

You take an advertising budget that is limited to begin with, then water it down further by pouring it out into six, seven, or 10 cups.

Is it any wonder that you see so little in the way of results?

Can you imagine a man trying to dig a swimming pool with a shovel? He starts a hole over here. Then he gets tired of that and starts one over there. Then does it again. Another hole over there. What would he have at the end of the day? A bunch of holes and no swimming pool.

That's the way many businesses spend their marketing budgets, digging tiny holes, starting and stopping, and ending up with nothing to show for it. You don't build an image or a brand this way.

What you need is an intelligent, workable, long-term system.

LET ME CHALLENGE SOME ASSUMPTIONS

First of all, who says that you have to reach *all* 100,000–200,000 or more people in your area, 100% of your market? How many people do you really need in order to have a thriving, growing business?

What would it mean to your business if you completely captured mental real estate in 10% of the population? That means a minimum of 10,000 people would think of you first whenever they had a desire or need for the product or service you offer, and have some kind of logical or emotional connection with you.

Second, who says it's best to use *all* the available vehicles of advertising? You'll never hear me say that, in fact, just the opposite! Most businesses are in too many cups!

What if you focused on *one* cup, put your available budget into it, and worked it consistently, over months and years? What if you pounded away consistently and frequently, dominating and drenching until you owned mental real estate and captured mindshare with that cup?

The great and amazing truth is that this is *doable.* To do it successfully, you need a clear-cut strategy and the focus to stay with it.

You need to apply your strategy-based message with consistency and frequency.

By *consistency* I mean picking a single cup and sticking with it for years and years. Absolutely no less than 52 weeks consecutively.

By *frequency* I mean continuing to fill that cup up. Your goal is to dominate that cup (or medium) to the point you *own the hearts and minds* of everyone in that cup.

Why do companies like State Farm and Geico continue pounding their message year after year? Because they know that there are always new people out there, and that they must continue to reinforce the message in those who've already heard it.

Why does McDonald's keep pouring it on? Because they know it costs much more to start over again to capture mental real estate than it does to maintain what they've got.

These companies are masters at being consistent and frequent. You can learn from them. They know a secret: This is more about psychology than advertising.

Advertising Blunder #3:
Microwave Mentality

Microwave mentality is the desire for "instant" advertising results. Isn't that consistent with the prevailing feeling of our culture? Microwaves aren't fast enough, even with the ability to produce a fully-baked potato in minutes instead of an hour. We'll stand impatiently by the microwave as it cooks in one-tenth of the time. It is with this same impatience that we manage our businesses. We want results NOW!

Here's an illustration of different ways to think about your marketing. Ask yourself which one better characterizes your perspective:

- *Marketing Microscope* — Short-term view for what is happening now. Simply concerned with "making the month."

- *Marketing Telescope* — "Big picture" view of the marketplace over an extended period of time. This is where you look not just at what is happening now, but well into the future.

These are two very different ways of operating a business. Microscope businesses are just concerned with here and now, with this week, this month. Telescope businesses say, "I don't want to be here in this same condition five years from now." With the Telescopic view, you can patiently work a long-term plan, sticking with it through years, and reap the benefits.

Look at it like investing. There are those known as day-traders. Their philosophy can be described this way:

Investors counting on short-term results, and often anxious to make changes.

Day traders jump around, looking for "quick profit" — buying and selling all day. Most advertisers are the same. "Let's try this. No, let's try that. No, here's a new thing." They jump from print, to radio, to direct mail, always looking for a quick fix, a quick pay-off. But how often does that pay off? By the way, in the last seven years, about three percent of day traders in America have made money. Wouldn't you like to do better?

We're always going to hit the speed bumps of business. Short-termers feel the pain, panic, and change plans all the time. With a long-term plan, you still hit the speed bumps, but you stay the course, keep working the plan, and confidently move forward.

Look at someone like Warren Buffet. When the big IT boom was on, he was questioned for staying out of it. After the whole thing collapsed in the dot-bomb debacle, people were calling him a genius. He's the ultimate example of someone who has a rational long-term strategy and works it consistently. He exemplifies the long-term philosophy:

Investors with long-term strategies are likely to remain confident and stay the course.

Who made more money in recent years, day traders or Warren Buffet's Berkshire Hathaway? The contrast is between Microwave Mentality and Steps of Faith and Discipline. Will you sprinkle your cash around aimlessly, looking for the quick hit, the quick fix, and the quick return? Or, will you choose the systematic approach that gives you a long-term, measurable ROI?

Have you noticed that anything that feels good for the short-term tends not to be good for us over the long run? While possibly harmless in small doses, those things tend to create worse and worse consequences as they are used more and more. Chocolate is a great example.

Things that are good for us seem to work the opposite way. We see no immediate return. Can I do a four-mile power walk and drop 20 pounds today and be in shape? Can I skip my meals today, and slim down to my college weight? Of course not. I have to make lifestyle changes, and repeat them day after day. Over weeks and months, the results will come.

My grandfather, Melvin C. Morsch, was a very successful farmer in Hinckley, Illinois. I remember watching him plant corn, DeKalb XL45, to be specific. Do you think he ever came back the next day or week to check progress, and complained, "This isn't working"? My grandfather had common sense. He knew there was a time lag between sowing and reaping.

It's our demand for instant gratification that's the dealbreaker. Isn't that why we cheat on diets? Isn't that why we bail out of exercise programs? Small business owners tend to do the same with advertising.

Branding requires "Sticktoitiveness." Time is the friend of branding, and one of the essential elements for working a successful strategy.

State Farm Insurance didn't brand "Like a good neighbor" into people's minds with a 13-week contract. They've been saying it for more than 30 years. When is the last time you committed to a long-term marketing plan, and let me be very clear — by long term, I am talking years?

A great brand is in it for the long haul.[5]
—Scott Bedbury,
former Starbucks and Nike
marketing executive

If you've been operating with the Microscope Mentality, it's time to try the Telescope approach with the commitment to a plan.

In order to capture mindshare, you need to understand how the human mind works. This is where it really gets good!

Breaking it Down

CHAPTER 5

- You will save valuable money in your ad budget if you avoid these three classic advertising blunders:

  1. Spending advertising dollars without knowing how you will measure the ROI.

  2. Watering down your message by trying to use too many different media — too many cups.

  3. The desire for instant advertising results.

- ***Branding happens over years*** ... not days, weeks, or months.

- I promise you, at least once in a good branding campaign, you will want to "bail out." Branding requires staying the course!

www.brandsformation.com

6

Getting on the Ladder

Word of mouth is the best form of advertising. People telling their friends and family how great your product or service is, right?

Well, yes and no. No one can argue against good word of mouth. Still, there are two inherent weaknesses to word of mouth advertising. First, you can't control exactly what's said. Second, it's typically very slow. You have no control over what is said or how fast it spreads.

Branding is taking word of mouth to the next level. **Branding is "controlled word of mouth advertising."** You control what is said about you. You determine what key words or phrases become attached to your business. And because you can control the frequency of the message, it is accelerated. Branding can get you there faster!

For years, Volvo has said "safety." For the public, Volvo = safety. State Farm has said "neighbor." For the public, State Farm = neighbor. Branding means you can control not only what is said, but even what is *thought* about you.

In order to understand how and why it works, it's important to understand some things about the human mind and memory. While some of the terminology might be new to you, the concepts are easily grasped — partly because you, as much as anyone else, have been a subject of others' efforts to capture mindshare.

UNDERSTANDING THE MINDS
YOU'RE TRYING TO REACH

This is where the pioneering work of Jack Trout has been so helpful. In 1981, Al Ries and Jack Trout wrote *Positioning: The Battle for Your Mind,* and it turned Madison Avenue upside down. Eleven books and hundreds of successful clients later, these are the points that Jack asserts about human minds[6]:

- Minds are *limited* — they can only remember a small number of units.
- Minds *hate confusion* — they are attracted to simplicity and order.
- Minds are *insecure* — which is why they are easily swayed by convincing authority.
- Minds *rarely change* — and because they find changes so difficult, much of our intelligence is devoted to rationalization, that is, coming up with rational explanations for our emotional decisions.
- Minds can *lose focus* — they are easily distracted and confused by vague communication or images.

Spend just a few minutes reflecting on the above points, and you will see some obvious applications. Chief among these will be the importance of *simplicity* in advertising.

Cowgill Dental Keeps You Smiling is a prime example of the principle on a local scale. Nobody wants to go to the dentist, but Dr. Cowgill's phrase puts the focus on something everybody does want. "Like a good neighbor, State Farm is there" is the same application on a national scale. Insurance is a complicated subject for most people; and, because it deals with trouble and disasters, people are reluctant to think about it. "Like a good neighbor" cuts right through the resistance with a positive image offering comfort and help. No wonder it has worked so well for so long.

UNDERSTANDING THE LADDER

Let's take a little test. Write down your answers to the following questions:

- How many brands of ***toothpaste*** can you name?
- How many ***rental car*** companies can you name?
- How many ***body wash*** brands can you name?

Maybe the most amazing thing associated with this quiz is the fact that I've been able to count roughly 37 brands of toothpaste, 14 rental car companies, and more than 150 brands of body washes available to the American consumer.

Even so, you are a rare individual if you can name more than seven items in each category. Most people run out of ideas after four or five, especially if they are limited to a minute or less. The top brands have captured mindshare on the first few rungs of the ladder, and all the rest are simply lost in the herd.

How many units of thought can the average mind deal with at one time? As a result of his research, Harvard psychologist George A. Miller concluded that the answer is seven.[7] Hearing of this a minister friend of mine responded, "That's right. Even regular churchgoers usually can't remember all of the Ten Commandments. If challenged to name them, they usually peter out after about six" — just as Dr. Miller says.

Do you know what this means to you as a business owner? *If you're not on the top three rungs, you're not even considered* when consumers are deciding where to go for the product or service that you offer.

You simply MUST have and work a strategy to get on that mental ladder in one of the top three positions.

SATURATED VERSUS OPEN LADDERS

The next thing you've got to determine is what ladder you're on. It makes a great deal of difference if your offering is in the category of a *Saturated* versus an *Open* Ladder. Let me define the terms:

A Saturated Ladder is one where most consumers can name businesses or products to fill the rungs. Banks are a good example. In a recent study in a Midwest market, all but nine percent of people surveyed could readily name a bank, and most could name several. That means mindshare has been captured already by others, and a new bank would have to find a way to wedge itself onto that ladder. It can be done, and we'll discuss how later.

An Open Ladder is a category where few people can name businesses or products in a certain category, and many can name none at all. This might be because it is a new product or service, or it might be because of the nature of the business. For example, in that same Midwest study, 71% of people could not name a chiropractor, and 52% could not name a dentist (makes you wonder about their dental health, doesn't it?). Services and semiprofessional services are often in the *Open Ladder* category, because people don't think about them until they have a current need.

These typically include, but are not limited to:
- Heating/Air Conditioning
- Fencing
- Roofing
- Chiropractors
- Plumbing
- Dentists and Cosmetic Dentists
- Attorneys

Open Ladders equal huge opportunity, because the first on a ladder typically owns it. An *Open Ladder* means the field is wide-open for the taking, to whoever gets there firstest with the mostest!

In a two-year period, Genesis Painting, a residential painter, jumped from 11% to 21% in mindshare. When asked, "Name the first painter that comes to mind," one in every five prospective customers now answers, "Genesis Painting." That has helped improve Genesis' sales. Meanwhile, their top competitor has dropped from 15% to eight percent. We don't know how it has affected their sales, but I could take a guess.

HOW MEMORY WORKS

We have five senses: sight, hearing, smell, taste, and touch. Each of them can be a source of memory. Knowing this, some advertisers have learned to appeal to more than one.

One of my favorite places in the world to sail to is Mackinac Island, off the northern tip of lower Michigan. It's like going back in time. Others obviously feel the same, because more than three million vacationers visit every summer. The movie *Somewhere in Time* was shot there (with Christopher Reeve and Jane Seymour). The producers picked an appropriate setting, because cars aren't even allowed on the island. All you hear are the clip-clop of horses pulling carriages on the old village streets.

The principal product sold there is fudge, which is why the locals refer to tourists as "fudgies." On one visit as I stood outside one of the fudge shops, I noticed what they were doing. Not only were they making their delicious concoction in full view of passersby, who could watch the whole process taking place on marble tables through massive glass windows, they had actually constructed blowers above the windows to send the fudge's aroma out over the sidewalk. Talk about sneaky! The combined senses of sight and smell made that fudge irresistible to those outside, and their sales proved it.

Even so, the principal ways we get programmed to recall advertising are usually through sight and sound. Our minds are truly amazing in their ability to retain implanted memories. Think about the illustration I shared earlier about Winston cigarettes. A huge percentage of people older than 45 today can instantly remember "Winston tastes good, like a cigarette should" — even though they have not heard it over television or radio *since 1970!* How can this be?

It helps to understand what neurologists call "iconic" and "echoic" memory.

Iconic memory refers to what comes in through sight. It comes from "icon" which means an image. Our sense of sight is so vivid and important to us, that you would think that it's the most important source of memories, but this is not true.

Echoic memory is the result of what we hear. Contrary to what most people would guess, what we hear is retained in our memories much longer and more accurately than what we see. Why? Because it takes up to five seconds to store sound, while sight is stored in one to two seconds. Since sound takes up to five times longer, it is far more accurate and far more easily recalled.

Insurance companies have conducted extensive research in this area. They are naturally very interested in how accurate eyewitness accounts of accidents are. They studied events witnessed by a number of people, and compared how much agreement there was based on what the people saw and heard. According to their findings, only 1.9 out of 10 people agreed on what they saw; six to seven out of 10 agreed on what they heard.

Helen Keller was blind and deaf since before her second birthday, basically cut off from the outside world until she met Annie Sullivan. Annie found a way to break through and open up her world. If anyone can compare the relative value of sight and sound, it would be Helen Keller. This is what she said:

> **The problems of deafness are deeper and more complex, if not more important, than those of blindness. Deafness is a much worse misfortune, for it means the loss of the most vital stimulus — the sound of the voice that brings language, sets thoughts astir, and keeps us in the intellectual company of man.**

Haven't you had the maddening experience of not being able to get a jingle or a song out of your head? The mind works by cues. That's why a whole song can be brought to mind by merely giving someone the first line. That's why most of us learned our ABCs through a song.

People say they can't memorize. All school teachers have heard the complaint, but they know better. Years after they last heard it, these same people "who can't memorize" can sing the rest of the song after being given the first line: "I wish I were an Oscar Meyer wiener … "

That's the power of echoic memory. That's why the United States government in 1970 outlawed cigarette ads involving sound. Cigarette companies found themselves at a severe disadvantage in their branding efforts as a result. Cigarette ads in magazines just don't carry the same punch as the rugged Marlboro Man backed by the theme from *The Magnificent Seven.* I'll even bet that from memories of old-time radio, your parents or grandparents can still tell you what "LSMFT" means. Ask them. ("Lucky Strike Means Fine Tobacco," the radio announcers said *ad nauseam*).

These are some of the reasons I'm such an advocate of advertising with intrusive media like TV and radio. Quoting Jack Trout once again, "People spend 85% of their time immersed in ear (broadcast) media, and only 15% with eye (print) media." So shoot where the ducks are flying.

Breaking it Down

CHAPTER 6

- Your goal is to own mental real estate — to get on the ladder in people's minds. When they think of you first, you have a huge competitive advantage.

- **Open Ladder:** Few people can name businesses or products in a certain category. This is the easier ladder for gaining and owning mental real estate.

- **Saturated Ladder:** A ladder where most people can name businesses or products in certain categories to fill the rungs. It's a little trickier to get on this ladder, but it can be done.

- Because people have a limited capacity for remembering, your goal is to occupy a place on the top three rungs of the ladder, preferably the top rung!

- Invest your money in intrusive media.

www.brandsformation.com

7

THE SYSTEM

The BrandsFormation™ System has four fundamentals:
- **Strategy**
- **A Strategy-Based Message**
- **Consistency**
- **Dominant Frequency**

Each of these fundamentals is important on its own; however, when combined in this "system" the synergy of the four creates a powerful and proven marketing tool that will Brandsform your business.

With that said, you simply can't apply BrandsFormation™ successfully without thoroughly understanding and developing your strategy. This is why I am dedicating this chapter to the first fundamental — Strategy.

Strategy is that "something" that makes your business individual, special and different. Great strategy is easy to understand and easy to communicate. It is a long-term plan of action designed to help you win. Strategy is about choice, and it affects the outcome of this system. Make your choices clear, honest, and simple. If you bumble on your strategy, your BrandsFormation™ will fail.

Before we dive into developing your strategy, I want to touch on the importance of a system, and how following a system works to your advantage.

THE VALUE OF A SYSTEM

During one of my seminars, I ran into a lady named Dawn. I was quite surprised at seeing her, because she looked dramatically different. Since my last visit to her town, Dawn had lost 37 pounds.

I asked her how she did it.

"That's easy," Dawn said proudly, "I have a system!" I must have looked puzzled, because she laughed and added, "My system is 2000, 98, 42, 21, 3!"

I naturally was curious and asked her to elaborate.

"I worked out a way of keeping my focus on my reachable goals. Each day they are 2000 calories, 98 protein, 42 carbs, 21 fat, and 3 times a week exercising. That's how I've lost 37 pounds. It helps me be accountable to myself."

That's what a system can do for you. It gives you an understandable, doable set of actions and goals to get you where you want to go.

A system means a process, a track to run on. It's like a formula in algebra. You plug the variables in the formula, and it helps you work out the answer. And when you have a proven system that works, you don't have to learn everything the hard way. You can learn from the accumulated wisdom and experience of others. It doesn't take away from your individuality or creativity. It gives a framework within which you can exercise those things to your heart's content.

You've got a payroll system, a hiring system, training systems ... I ask you again: Doesn't it make sense to have a marketing system?

As I said in the first chapter, it's like following the rules of sailing. It's dangerous to go out onto open water if you're just sailing by the seat of your pants. The rules of proper sailing don't stifle your spirit of adventure; they keep you safe and headed in the right direction as you live your spirit of adventure out on the water.

THE SYSTEM: PART 1

STRATEGY

Most of your hard thinking and work will be devoted to this first part. Strategy is hard work, which is why few people are good at it. Coming up with your strategy will require you to determine your answers in three areas.

In 2003, Jack Trout granted an interview, in which he shared many insightful points.[8] He said there are three steps to building a good business strategy, and elaborated on each. The rest of this chapter is built on his three steps and explanatory comments.

1. **"Understand Your Competition in the Marketplace."**
This may surprise you, but you don't start with you. You begin by taking stock of the competitive world around you. Ask and answer regarding your competition:

- Who's out there? Who else is on the mental ladder already? Is there a market leader?
- What are they doing?
- Are they strong or weak?
- Is the Marketing Ladder Open or Saturated?
- Is there a gap where I can wedge myself in?

These questions not only make you sharply aware of your competitors, but they also prepare you for the second part of strategy:

2. **"Determine Your Differentiating Idea, and Prove It."**
- Is there an idea I can "own"?
- Can I be a specialist? A pioneer?

To help you find your *Differentiating Idea*, let me recall some of the key questions presented earlier:

From your customer's perspective:
- What will your product or service DO FOR ME?
- Why should I go to you instead of your competition?
- What's different and better about your product or service?

From your standpoint:
- Who are our customers?
- What do they want?
- How can I prove or demonstrate my Differentiating Idea?

ANALYZE AND DIFFERENTIATE

When Papa John's Pizza was trying to figure out how to break into the pizza market, pizza was by no means a new product in America. This is a great example of differentiation, and an easy one for people to grasp. You have several large national chains, and countless local mom & pop pizza shops. Beginning with the competition, they asked who already owned mental real estate. The mental ladder looked something like this:

WHO?	MINDSHARE?
Pizza Hut	Family-oriented
Domino's	Home-delivery
Little Caesar's	Two-for-One / low price
Local Mom & Pops	Familiarity? Quality?

Now Papa John's asked the question of differentiation: "How can we stand out as different? What's left?" Family? Taken. Delivery? Taken. Cheap? Taken.

They arrived at the realization that TASTE was wide-open. They built a strategy around "Better Ingredients. Better Pizza."[9]

The result? *Papa John's was the fastest growing franchise in the United States several years running!*

They analyzed, they differentiated, they conquered! You can do the same with your business.

SAVED BY RETURNING TO BASICS

The most successful companies can stray from the basics and lose their place. Here's an example of one that did, but was able to turn it around.

Burger King went through a terrible period, as shown by its record of having 10 different CEOs in 14 years. At the end of that string, four out of their top 10 franchises filed bankruptcy. The once-thriving company almost fell to third behind Wendy's.

Burger King's new CEO, Greg Brenneman, came in and did his analysis. He asked one of the fundamental questions: "Who is our customer?" He discovered a striking statistic: 18% of Burger King customers were responsible for 48% of their sales. In other words, their loyal fan base was *really* loyal, and loved to consume mass quantities. The typical BK customer was an 18- to 34-year-old male.

Burger King decided to focus on this group, their "superfans." Despite whether or not it was considered politically correct in this culture, they targeted this group of young men who wanted their meals the mega-sized old fashioned way, calories be damned.

Burger King turned it around successfully. In 2005 they registered their biggest gain in 21 years.[10]

TAN PARKER: TEXAS STATE REPRESENTATIVE

BrandsFormation™ works because it focuses like a laser beam on great strategy. There are many good businesses out there that are struggling because they haven't found their strategy, their story, and/or they don't know how to communicate it.

Case and point: Tan Parker, a great guy who, for most of his life, has been involved in politics in many ways including participating in numerous local, state and national campaigns. Even Ronald Reagan was impressed in a one-on-one meeting with the young, enthusiastic and determined Tan Parker. Sounds like a guy who could breeze through any election, right? Well, like any good business, and politics is definitely a business, you must have a great strategy.

Let me set the stage: The 13-year incumbent made the announcement that she would not be seeking reelection. Tan, along with four others, threw their hats into a five-way, hotly contested, Republican primary battle for Texas State Representative.

Having never sought or held public office before, Tan was the complete unknown. His opponents were a former mayor, a current mayor, a former school board president and now local realtor, and a well-known and respected local businessman.

Tan's challenge was to get voters to think of him when they went to "pull the lever." How would he stand out amongst the other four better-known Republicans? First, Tan put a great team in place that included my wife, Roann. Many meetings were held using my office as what became known as the "war room" during the campaign.

As the race rolled on and heated up, the winner was anyone's call. Who would end up with the prize? As Tan and his team plugged away, I tried my best to stay out of it, but I couldn't help myself. I could see one thing that definitely set Tan apart from the pack that wasn't being communicated effectively.

He had the endorsement of one of the most well-known and respected Republicans in America, former United States House of Representatives Majority Leader, Dick Armey!

The distinction was clear, and we knew this would give people a reason to vote for Tan that no one else could claim. Since he was the least well-known of all of the candidates, Mr. Armey's endorsement would help to set him apart and raise awareness for Tan by linking him to someone that everybody knew. Tan was Dick's pick and we knew it could elevate his campaign and set him apart if communicated effectively to the voters.

The challenge became how to get that strategy into the "minds" and hence votes of these potential Republican primary voters? Looking back, the answer seemed simple enough, but it didn't hit me until I was driving down the road one afternoon.

Every candidate had 4-foot by 8-foot campaign signs positioned all over the district and Tan was no exception. We simply went to the local sign guy and had him print up two-foot by four-foot stick-on bright yellow mini-banners and plastered them on the corner of each of the large campaign signs all over the Texas countryside. On those mini-banners we simply printed these four words: "Endorsed by Dick Armey."

That following January, we were pleased to be able to attend the inauguration and sit in the Texas House of Representatives and watch as Tan was sworn in by the Texas Secretary of State. Way to go Tan ... we know you'll do great things!

There is always something that sets you apart from your competition. In Tan's case, one glaring difference was a big name endorsement. Strategically using Dick's endorsement helped voters to make a distinction and a decision. Find out what sets you apart. Give people a reason to "vote for you."

WHAT'S YOUR DIFFERENTIATING IDEA?

Here are some points and questions to help you determine your *Differentiating Idea.*

- Find something you do very well and build your reputation around it.
- Don't try to be all things to all people. You undermine your product or service if you try to be everything to everyone. That's the lesson of the Burger King story. They bounced back when they quit that effort, and went after their core fans.
- Dramatize your *Differentiating Idea.* Ask, "How can I bring my message to life?" Build it around the question every consumer is asking: "What will your product or service do for me?"
- Words are what get stuck in the mind. You are on your way if you can own a single word or a short phrase in the minds of people. Volvo = "safety." BMW = "drive."
- Even if you are selling a product that is purchased emotionally, you must give people a logical reason, a rationalization, for why they "need" it. Nobody really "needs" a Rolex or a Mercedes. The person who buys one feels much better about themselves by focusing on the "quality workmanship" of their emotionally-driven purchase.
- How are you going to PROVE your *Differentiating Idea?* Hard data? Research? Surveys? Testimonials?

There must be criteria to provide a litmus test to discern a good strategy. There are two:

1. Do you have a genuine *Differentiating Idea?*

2. Is it a reason to buy your product or service?

The answer to both questions must be *yes* in order to be a great Strategy.

Jack's parting interview shot was simple and to the point. "You must either have a point of difference or a very low price." That's why one of his books is called, *"Differentiate or Die."*

Now, let's take a look at the third step to building a good business strategy.

3. **"Have a communications program in place."**

You're almost there. Now you've got to have a rational plan for getting your message out. Here's where we'll use some of the philosophy we discussed previously, illustrated by the pitcher of water and cups. Instead of spreading your ad budget all around, inadequately servicing six, seven, or eight avenues of advertising, choose one cup, fill it up, and measure the ROI. Only then add cup #2. It's better to dominate a single cup, where you can pound away with your message against the same group of people and thoroughly capture mindshare, than to spread yourself over seven or eight cups and have no dominance to show for it.

Most do a little bit here, a little bit there, a little bit over there. The little bit method doesn't work. They "little bit" themselves to death. As my former partner Phil Fisher says, "It's like taking a leak in the ocean and expecting the water to rise."

By now, you should have a start on your Strategy. We'll cover the remaining three BrandsFormation™ fundamentals in the next chapter.

Breaking it Down

CHAPTER 7

- Fundamentals of the BrandsFormation™ System
  - ✔ Strategy
  - ✔ A Strategy-based message
  - ✔ Consistency
  - ✔ Dominant Frequency

- Good strategy never starts with you. It starts with your competition!

- Understand your competition.

- Determine your *Differentiating Idea (DI)*, and prove it. Don't try to be all things to all people. Make your DI bigger than life.

  Your *Differentiating Idea* must give people a reason to buy.

- Everyone has something or several things that set them apart from the competition. Find what sets you apart and give people a reason to do business with you.

- Put your money in one place/one cup and dominate that cup! Measure the ROI, and only then, add another cup.

www.brandsformation.com

8

The SYSTEM, continued

Once you have determined your strategy, the next step
is to find a way to drive it into the minds of people. This is
where you develop and apply a Strategy-Based Message.

"LOOK, MA, NO CAVITIES!"

There are more than 35 brands of toothpaste on the
market in America today. Why should anyone pick yours
for brushing their "pearly-whites"?

That was the question faced by the makers of *Crest.*
Colgate was the giant. They had introduced their first
toothpaste in 1873, and the first toothpaste in a tube in
1896. In the 1950s, when *Crest* was trying to break
through, *Colgate* was the clear tenant on the top rung of
the ladder. At the time, they were using the word
"cleaner," in fact, three ways: cleaner breath, cleaner taste,
and cleaner teeth.

Some marketing genius realized the idea of *cavity*

protection was wide open. Their strategy was set, and they aimed their appeal at moms. If you are in your 40s or older, you probably remember the excited kid running to his mom's arms from the dentist's office exclaiming, "Look, Ma, no cavities!"

That was followed by a man in an official-looking white coat reciting the statement proudly inscribed on every box and tube of *Crest*. The American Dental Association's verdict was, "Crest has been shown to be an effective decay-preventive dentifrice that can be of significant value when used as directed in a conscientiously applied program of oral hygiene and regular professional care." Boy, that sure sounded impressive!

The funny thing about it is that any fluoride toothpaste of basic value could have claimed the same statement from the ADA. Today others do, but it's way too late. *Crest* made the phrase "cavity protection" theirs!

THE SYSTEM: PART 2

A STRATEGY-BASED MESSAGE

The *Crest* phrase, *"Look Ma … No cavities!"*, is a prime example of a Strategy-Based Message. However you come at it, your strategy is to identify your Differentiating Idea, and then develop a strategy-based message so you can drive your strategy into consumers' minds. Your goal is connection. *How can you connect with people?* What words and ideas can you use to capture mindshare?

We begin by working to uncover your unique story. So often, business owners have said to me, "I don't have a story."

"Yes, you do," I always insist. "You just haven't uncovered it." I dig and probe to find out what drives them as entrepreneurs or service providers. There are always passions, commitments, and values beneath the surface, which the business owners have taken for granted. There are great people building good businesses in America! Bringing to light the uniqueness of this country's small businesses is one of the great pleasures of my work.

Second, I ask you to analyze what your competition is doing: Who's on the ladder? How do they promote themselves? What angles are open for attack?

Then the big question: What will set you apart, what will differentiate you from the pack? How will you carve your way onto the ladder? What do you bring to the table that speaks to what your product or service will do for your customers or clients? Where do you fit on their mental ladder?

SAYING IT WITHOUT SAYING IT

Dr. Terry Cowgill was the new kid on the block. He was up against many established dentists. How would he build up a brand new practice?

He decided he would try something that most dentists frowned upon, advertising. Dr. Cowgill knew if he was going to put several hundred thousand dollars into a new practice, and get a good return on his investment, he had to do something different.

Because most people have negative associations about going to the dentist, Dr. Cowgill's strategy was to be the dentist that people associate with fun — NOT drills, cavities, pain, fear and dread!

Instead he wanted to be known as the dentist with a sense of humor, the dentist that makes you smile. He knew if he could make you laugh or smile, his chances would improve greatly that you would want to see him as your dentist. How could he say it without saying it? Strategist and good friend, Theresa Timm came up with the idea to sponsor a humorous radio show called, *The Adventures of the Tooth Fairy*. That particular sponsorship ended more than 10 years ago and people still ask him today about the Tooth Fairy. Dr. Cowgill is now producing his own parody ads that are unique and have been extremely successful. He said, "People tell me they look forward to our new ads."

Dr. Cowgill started with a five-year plan that included no payments to himself. Within seven months, he threw it out because things were so far ahead of pace. Dr. Cowgill's strategy worked because he "filled one cup," in this case radio, and he pounded his message again and again. He was able to show people through humor and self-deprecation that he was a different kind of dentist.

He built a stand-alone office during his third year in business. And he did it right by extending his brand of *fun and smiles* into his building. When you walk in you know you are not in the typical dental office. It is the *Taj Mahal* of dental offices with 12 treatment rooms, fireplace, beautiful décor, and a great play area designed for children.

Now when people are looking for a dentist in his area, they think of Dr. Cowgill, the dentist that keeps you smiling!

DIFFERENTIATE AND DRAMATIZE

Don "Opie" Opheim is the owner of a good heating and air conditioning business. He had been in business for several years and had good "word of mouth." While word of mouth is one of the best forms of advertising, it has its challenges, one being that it typically works at a very slow pace. Opie wanted to kick it up and accelerate the progress — he wanted *everyone* to think of him first when they needed the services he offered.

My friend and co-strategist, Pat Ebertz, went to work digging for his story. He discovered Opie's unusual commitment to the customer. They guarantee that they will be at your house within a one-hour window. Bingo ... a strategy was born! With most home service providers, whether it's HVAC, cable TV, carpet cleaning or phone repair — you are given a large window of time where you have to wait for them to show up. You've heard it, "Yeah, we can be there sometime between 9 a.m. and 1 p.m." For most of us, being trapped in our home for the day just because some guy can't do a little time management is not an option.

The strategy for Opie's was set: They would be the *heating and air conditioning guys that will always be at your home within a 60-minute window.*

The strategy-based message became, "If we're not on time, you don't pay a dime." Opie has become the "on-time guy" in people's minds. He is the friend in the heating and air conditioning business who understands his customer's time constraints. He is the guy that works on behalf of your schedule, and most importantly — it's not just words, he backs it up.

Opie's message is anything but forgettable. He voices all of his commercials, and has become quite popular for his bad singing. His commercials are funny, self-deprecating and honest.

This year, Opie's Heating and Air Conditioning is expected to double their sales compared to just three years ago. Opie's BrandsFormation™ is working!

Neither Dr. Cowgill or Opie are marketers by trade, but they are smart. They understand the importance of humor. Everyone likes a good laugh for the right reasons. By being funny, they are actually bonding with potential customers.

Stories and humor get past people's defenses and carry an emotional appeal. According to Scott Bedbury, "Emotions drive most, if not all, of our decisions." But always remember: people buy emotionally, but they justify logically. Therefore, even though you might have a strong emotional appeal, you will always want to include logical reasons to help the buyer justify his purchase. Won't that be rationalizing? Yes, but there wouldn't be many Rolexes, Mercedes, or $100,000 boats purchased without it.

A STRATEGY THAT HELPED
IN A RAGING TIDE

In the late '90s, realizing his current career wasn't making him happy, John Meyer took a big leap of faith and bought his own business, State Street Mortgage.

Combined with John's skillful leadership and the record low interest rates of the "re-fi" boom during the early 2000s, State Street was doing great by any standard. Still, John knew there was more to do to ensure the long-term success of his business.

In 2005, John hired my firm to go to the next level. He wanted the same thing all business owners want — more customers, financial success and long-term stability. We set out to do just that.

We developed a strategy and created a series of commercials built around the "The Mortgage Man" and a custom jingle done in the same style as the muffin man melody. We use different bricks in every commercial, but always the same mortar, *The Mortgage Man*, and always the same jingle in every commercial.

In 2007 the Mortgage business hit the skids. More than 20,000 people lost their jobs, the entire industry has shrunk by 30-to-50%, and there arc still tremors.

While many have had to close up shop, State Street Mortgage is still moving forward and standing firm in their long-term plan. John credits his survival, in large part, to BrandsFormation™. He said it has helped to insulate him against a tidal wave of Tsunami-type proportions that washed over his industry.

THE SYSTEM: PART 3

CONSISTENCY

You are after a consistent message, no matter what, where, or when you say it. In all media — print, website, online, direct mail, signage, radio, television — you look, sound, and feel the same to the consumer. You want them to identify you in split-second time.

Breaking it down, consistency means:
1. **Look** consistency — colors, logos, graphics, fonts.
2. **Sound** consistency — music, voice, tone, inflections, words.
3. **Media** consistency — instead of jumping around from cup to cup, you've chosen to dominate one media cup and fill it up before moving on and adding a second and third cup.
4. **Time** consistency — measured not in weeks or months, but in years.

Your commitment must be to STICK WITH IT. Be determined to work your marketing plan for the long haul. Anything less than years in duration isn't branding.

> **A brand is not built overnight.**
> **Success is measured in decades, not years.**[11]
> — *Al Ries and Laura Ries*

Consistency means you keep hammering away at your *Differentiating Idea* — while maintaining interest through changing stories, AND remaining instantly identifiable. Many small business people have become local celebrities through exactly this method. As the famous poet Henry Wadsworth Longfellow said, "If you only knock long enough and loud enough at the gate, you are sure to wake up somebody."

THE SYSTEM: PART 4

DOMINANT FREQUENCY

If you can't be a dominant player in a particular

medium — Get out! This is, again, where you apply the lessons you learned with the water pitcher and cups. Remember, your goal is not to spread your budget around many forms of advertising, but to choose one cup, one avenue of advertising, and dominate it. Even with a limited budget, you can dominate a single medium, become one of the biggest voices on that station or program, and get your message into the minds of consumers — if you plot wisely.

DON'S TOWING

Remember our friend, Don, the steady and honest owner of a tow-truck company, known as — you guessed it — "Don's Towing"? Don has a great heart, and a good towing business he built over time.

Year after year, Don advertised in his local *Yellow Pages*. When there was only one book and he was the dominant player, life was good. Challenges began when *Yellow Pages* started publishing multiple books, and Don's competitors grew to more than 20. Besides that, when a person's car breaks down on the side of the road, they don't usually have a copy of the *Yellow Pages* handy to look up Don's ad.

Don made a decision to grow his company. He realized he could consistently pound his message into the minds of potential customers and get his name on their mental ladder. Then, when they did break down, the first person they would think of is — you guessed it — Don's Towing.

So, he took the bulk of his $48,000 out of "passive" *Yellow Pages*, and decided to go dominate radio. Now, instead of waiting for people to break down and hoping they somehow find him among the 20 other "hockey pucks" who also say they tow, Don has changed the rules of the game. Today, people know "Don's Towing" before "the need for a tow" even arises. How? Because every single day, Don is out there telling his story: "Hi … I'm Don. I hope you never have to need us, but if you do, I'm AAA certified. Be sure to ask for Don's!"

He speaks in a monotone, little inflection and no excitement — but obviously very genuine. But then, the next day it's, "Hi … I'm Don … "

The next day: "Hi … I'm Don … " The next day: "Hi … I'm Don … "

The next day: "Hi … I'm Don … " The next day: "Hi … I'm Don … "

The next day: "Hi … I'm Don … " The next day: "Hi … I'm Don … "

The next day: "Hi … I'm Don … " The next day: "Hi … I'm Don … "

The next day: "Hi … I'm Don … " The next day: "Hi … I'm Don … "

The next day: "Hi … I'm Don … " The next day: "Hi … I'm Don … "

The next day: "Hi … I'm Don … " The next day: "Hi … I'm Don … "

The next day: "Hi … I'm Don … " The next day: "Hi … I'm Don … "

The next day: "Hi … I'm Don … " The next day: "Hi … I'm Don … "

The next day: "Hi … I'm Don … " The next day: "Hi … I'm Don … "

The next day: "Hi … I'm Don … " The next day: "Hi … I'm Don … "

The next day: "Hi ... I'm Don ... " The next day: "Hi ... I'm Don ... "

The next day: "Hi ... I'm Don ... " The next day: "Hi ... I'm Don ... "

Get the picture? That's what I call DOMINANT FREQUENCY! Don has gone from seven employees to 15 and counting, and he is now "Don's Towing and Auto Repair."

Another BrandsFormation™ success!

WORKING THE SYSTEM FOR YOU

Others can help you here. You don't have to be an expert on the details of broadcasting; you just have to be committed to The System and be determined to use Dominant Frequency.

Our world is constantly changing, and that will affect what are the best means of advertising. Who knows what changes are coming? Will the Internet make broadcast media obsolete in the next 20 years? Will TiVo kill television ads? I recently heard of some young people getting together to watch a month's worth of their favorite program, "The Office," in TiVo parties, because it cuts hours of watching TV down to minutes by zapping all the ads.

Heck, my neighbor Matt and I recently watched an entire Packers football game in under 25 minutes by zapping out anything that wasn't "playtime." Things are changing, so just be aware.

To conclude this chapter and the Four Fundamentals of BrandsFormation™, I recommend that you take some time to think about the things that make you different from your competition. Uncover your unique story, your differentiating idea, and remember to make it easy for people to understand and connect to. Next, look at the available media — again, I prefer broadcast or sound media — but the main point is whatever media you choose, you must be able to dominate it. Then, start pounding your message day-in and day-out in the minds of consumers and never stop!

Breaking it Down

CHAPTER 8

- **Strategy-Based Message.** Begin to develop your message by working to uncover your unique story. Everybody has one!

- You want your message to *connect with people*. Stories are the secret to getting past the "standard junk" filter.

- Be honest. Don't make claims you can't back up. Don't force something to fit – make the fit comfortable and easy for the consumer to understand.

- Stay away from words that anyone can claim ... quality, service, the best. *"Try to say it without saying it."*

- **Consistency:** You must be consistent, no matter what, where, or when you say it. You want people to be able to identify you in split-second time. Your website should be consistent with your radio message, for example.

- **Dominant Frequency:** You must dominate whatever intrusive media you choose. Then pound your message day in and day out in that "one cup" — and *never stop*!

www.brandsformation.com

9

BrandsFormation™ at Work

We teach a process I call "bricks & mortar" to business owners. It's simply a way to take your strategy and turn it into a strategy-based message.

You want to be the business that people think of first, whenever they need your product or service. Bricks & mortar connect a person's mind to your business.

There are two parts:

The MORTAR is the consistency of elements in your marketing message. The mortar serves to "cement" all the BRICKS together in a person's mind. Color gives your business a consistent look that ties everything together. Music gives your business a consistent sound (think jingles). Likewise, your business logo is a consistent look where it is applied to your building, vehicles, website, and such. Your voice or another consistent voice is your "audio logo." Again, these **mortar** elements give your brand a consistent look and sound. Most importantly, whether it is sight, sound, or strategy words — these mortar elements

rarely change. That's why you don't see the McDonald's "pink arches." They've been golden for 50 years. That's consistent.

The **bricks**, on the other hand, are **always changing**. The bricks are all the parts of your story that you build in the listener's mind, brick by brick, dramatizing what sets you apart. The most powerful bricks are always "stories" or parables. Most business owners have great stories to tell about themselves and their customers. They just aren't telling them.

THE POWER OF STORIES

Stories — the bricks — pack the punch. Stories give power to your message. Stories are what people remember, how they connect, and what enable you to get "stuck in their minds." Through stories you dramatize your company's difference and bring it to life. Through the use of stories you avoid the deadly hack clichés everybody talks about when asked, "What makes you different?" Products, service, selection, price. When clients tell me those things are their *Differentiating Idea*, I usually reply, "The last ten thousand guys I talked to said the same thing. Everybody says that stuff. What do you have that's different?" *Stories are the secret* to getting through and getting in.

Why do I put such an emphasis on stories? Because stories are how people think, remember, and communicate, and by which they are motivated and connected. People dislike advertising, but we all like stories. Stories so permeate our everyday speech that we are hardly aware of it. But try it. Go through a day and notice the allusions and stories you naturally use.

Stories are powerful, and your stories will help you communicate your message to your prospective customers.

AN ILLUSTRATION IS WORTH A THOUSAND WORDS

Let me share at length two real-life case studies that show how we work through "brandsforming" a business into a great local brand.

Don't get caught up in all the details. Every business is as unique as an individual person, and deals with its own mix of product or service, location, culture, and competition. The important point is not that you try to copy another company's marketing plan, but rather that you learn the process of working from your analysis through strategy to implementation. A great strategy is unique to the business. It can't be transferred, because it's not your story.

With that word of caution, read ahead and learn from others who have worked the BrandsFormation™ System before you.

BRANDSFORMATION™ AT WORK

Digital Print Ink ("d.p.i.")

Dave and Joy Adams started a Kwik Kopy franchise in 1979 in a strip mall. They broke even in three months, and continued to grow. It evolved into a full-service printer handling the bigger jobs that involve design, layout, mail merge, variable data, and specialty items like posters. At the time we began our analysis, they had just dropped their franchise name and changed their name to d.p.i.

Their primary competition was FedEx/Kinko's. Other printers had also been competing in the local market, but with no brand identity to speak of.

One interesting feature in Dave's background proved useful. While serving with the Army in Vietnam, Dave was the Community Relations Officer. That meant that anytime people in the Vietnamese village needed something, they went to Dave. This made him quite popular, and the villagers called him, "Di-We" — basically, Vietnamese for "Go-to Guy." It was still Dave's nickname in his inner circle. Just as Dr. Cowgill positioned himself as *the fun dentist with his smile campaign,* we could present Dave as "Di-We — your 'go-to guy' for printing." He'll get it done for you.

In addition to these points, our research indicated that cost, speed, and quality were the main criteria considered when consumers were selecting a printer.

Following the System, we first examined the competition on the Marketing Ladder and did our S.W.O.T. analysis (strengths, weaknesses, opportunities, and threats). This is what we found.

d.p.i. S.W.O.T. Analysis

STRENGTHS	WEAKNESSES
Quick	No outside sales
Quality	Low-priced competition
Commitment	Old Kwik Kopy image

Reputation	Name not getting out
Value	Location/walk-ins
Experts	
People who care	

OPPORTUNITIES	**THREATS**
Mailing (merges)	Mature industry
Variable data	Flat sales
Copying growth	Time
Brand strength	Loss of key people
Target marketing	FedEx/Kinko's
One-stop shop	Not being proactive
Graphic design	Insufficient backup
File handling expertise	

d.p.i. Strategy

We decided that no one wants or even needs a print job. Instead, it's what a good print job does for any business. All good businesses want their print jobs to make them "look great." Since FedEx/Kinko's occupied the top rung on the ladder, we thought our best bet was to reposition the competition. A common complaint Dave and Joy heard from former FedEx/Kinko's customers in the Springfield market was they were unhappy with poor quality and mistakes. They felt their print jobs were not checked for quality assurance, and that the staff was indifferent to their concerns. d.p.i. set out to differentiate themselves, and play to their own strengths by saying, "At d.p.i., we make you look great."

- Why do we make a business "Look great"?
- Position d.p.i. as the QUALITY alternative.

- Position d.p.i. as the competitive professional alternative with <u>FAST</u> turnaround and <u>QUALITY</u> print jobs, every time.
- Position d.p.i. as the printer that cares about the customer by making a solid commitment to the end result — quality print jobs.

I should add that while we were doing this marketing planning, we were also addressing other needs in the areas of performance, such as formalizing systems, and hiring a sales force.

d.p.i. Strategy-Based Message

MORTAR (consistent in all messages)
- Strategy words: "d.p.i. We make you look great!"
- Voice: Dave and/or Joy (the owners) the voice in every ad.
- Music: d.p.i. musical image.

Full Strategy Wedge:
"Digital Print Ink — not like those big, cold, 'take a number' quick print copy shops, where quality often suffers. Take the 'kinks' out of your printing and GO DIGITAL — d.p.i. We make you look great!"

[Remember: "Mortar" refers to the elements in the ads that never change. They are the same regardless of which bricks are highlighted.]

BRICKS (always changing)
We spent considerable time determining the "Why us instead of them?" question. From those conversations, we identified the following ideas we could use as "bricks."

The idea is to focus on one brick per ad, with the mortar remaining consistently the same.

- ✔ "Di-We" — Dave's story
- ✔ Speed
- ✔ Details
- ✔ Creative Department
- ✔ Delivery
- ✔ "Look"/Quality
- ✔ Turn-Key
- ✔ Creative

d.p.i. Radio Ad #1

Name: "Di-We"
Brick: Dave's story

Dave   My rich uncle, Sam, got me my first job right out of college. It was called the US Army, [pause] … their Vietnam "branch." I was the Community Relations Officer. The locals called me "Di-We." Whenever they came to me, I fixed them up.

Voices   Di-We! Di-We!

Dave   Got you covered, Dude! Look in your oxcart.

Voices   Rock on, Di-We! You da man!

Joy   Well, things haven't changed much, except he married me and we run Springfield's best print shop, d.p.i. — Digital Print Ink. Today, people still come in and call out, "Di-We!" and Dave gets them whatever they need. Whether it's 5,000 copies in a nanosecond, or a classy new four-color brochure, we're quick and we're very good.

Dave "Di-We" ... Isn't that Vietnamese for "Digital Dave"?

Joy Yeah, Vietnamese for "Play that funky music, Print Boy!"

Dave We're d.p.i. — Digital Print Ink. Professional business printers. Not like those big, cold, "take a number" quick copy and print shops where quality suffers.

Joy Take the KINKS out of your next print job, and go DIGITAL.

Dave d.p.i. — Digital Print Ink. Just south of Walnut Lawn on S. Campbell.

[jingle out . . .]

Jingle **"Digital Print Ink — We make you look great"**

d.p.i. Radio Ad #2

Name: "Picky"
Brick: "Details"

Joy	Some people were born RICH! Some people were born POOR!
Dave	I was born PICKY!
Joy	As a kid, "Di-We" Dave made his GI Joe action figures go through "spit shine" inspection.
Dave	"Cookie crumbs in your helmet!? Drop and give me 20, soldier!"
Joy	Dave didn't stop at soldiers. Oh, no! He was picky about cars, picky about food, picky about everything! This guy is just plain PICKY!
Dave	Then we opened our printing business ...
Joy	... and Dave took PICKY to a whole new level!
Dave	You want a PICKY printer that protects your image! Any mistake makes you look bad, so it has to be done right, down to the pickiest details.
Joy	So Dave taught everyone at d.p.i. to be PICKY.
Dave	We're d.p.i. — Digital Print Ink. Professional business printers. Not like those big, cold, "take a number" quick copy and print shops, where quality suffers.
Joy	Take the KINKS out of your next print job, and go DIGITAL for a better price!

Dave d.p.i. — Digital Print Ink. South of Walnut Lawn on S. Campbell.

Dave d.p.i. — the pickiest people in the printing profession.

Joy Precisely!

[jingle out . . .]

Jingle **"Digital Print Ink — We make you look great"**

Another BrandsFormation™!
d.p.i. experienced their BrandsFormation™. They had one of their best ever sales years, following a three-year decline. In fact, it worked so well that Dave and Joy sold d.p.i. to retire and became full-time grandparents.

BRANDSFORMATION™ AT WORK

Hangers Cleaners

Carl Rohman had been in the dry cleaning business for years. Originally, his business was known as Globe Cleaners, and their methods were conventional. Trying to break new ground, he made a substantial investment in new technology, a process using liquid CO_2. As he explained the new method, it was the difference between really clean versus wearing clothes that had been boiled in human sweat. That's right: "human sweat." He had our attention.

Talking to Carl, our team had the undeniable impression we were listening to someone who really cared about dry cleaning. It was simply his thing. He sold us on the benefits of his method. Carl's enthusiasm and knowledge was a brick we could build with: He became "Carl the dry cleaning geek."

Market Analysis

Even with his expensive technological advantage, Carl's sales were flat, and dry cleaning as a whole was a shrinking market. Nationally, the dry cleaning industry had been shrinking three percent to four percent each year since 2000, and was projected to continue in that direction. There were several reasons:

- More casual dress styles, even in professional arenas
- Better garment quality, that is, wash and wear
- Better home washing and drying machines
- Less expensive silk available from Chinese imports
- Demographic changes, as the population ages

Carl faced one major competitor who owned 40% of the market, and had a long-time image as the "quality" dry cleaner. They had slightly better geographic convenience than Hangers, and the advantage of offering "dry cleaning to your door." Another competitor had only two stores, but they were in excellent locations. There were several other single-store cleaners.

Research Overview
General Conclusions & Insights:

- Less than one-third of current customers seem to know the advantages of CO_2 or that Hangers offers

a different way to dry clean.
- Most people choose their dry cleaner on *convenience of location* — either to or from work.
- People who have had a bad experience don't "forgive and forget" — they become evangelists for their bad experience.

Hangers Cleaners Strategy

CO_2 was clearly his *Differentiating Idea*. No one else had it. And there were lots of potential bricks.
- Carl is an expert
- No heat
- No smell
- Less fading
- Less shrinking
- Easier on your clothes, so they last longer
- Better for the environment

Hangers Strategy-Based Message

MORTAR
- Strategy words: "Hangers' exclusive Kool Klean. No heat means brighter, fresher, longer-lasting, and just plain happier clothes. Kool Klean. Simply a better way to dry clean."
- Voice: Carl (owner)
- Music: Friendly, whistle

BRICKS

All these points make great stories/ bricks, and ways to dramatize the Kool Klean difference.
- "Need my pants for the trip" story

- No-fading story
- Longer-lasting story (almost lintless)
- No-smell story (smoke is liquid)
- No-heat story
- Less-shrinking story
- "Attention tag" challenge
- Route service advantages

Here's one sample ad based on our first brick, Carl as the "dry cleaning geek."

Hangers Radio Ad

Writer: Rob Barlow
Campaign: "Better Way to Clean"
Brick: "Geek"

[music under the VO]

Carl   Looking back now, I know I couldn't have escaped it. At first, I blamed it on the fact that my family's been in the business since the 1880s. But in the end, I knew it was my destiny.

                 Oh, I tried to fight it. Got a degree in Industrial Engineering, became a lawyer, then got a Masters in Business. Finally, I had to face the truth: I'm a dry cleaning geek.

                 First I bought Globe Cleaners. But 15 years later, my passion for dry cleaning led me to a better, more environmentally friendly way to clean clothes — Liquid CO_2. It's the Kool Klean. No heat. No shrinking. No kidding.

And that's when Globe Cleaners became Hangers Cleaners. Seven years later, and I'm still on a mission to find the best way to clean your clothes — one suit, shirt, blouse, and dress at a time.

I can't help it. I'm Carl Rohman, and I'm a dry cleaning geek.

Anncr.   Hangers' exclusive Kool Klean. No heat means brighter, fresher, longer-lasting — and just plain happier clothes. Kool Klean. Simply a better way to dry clean.

Carl   Frankly, I don't know why anyone would clean their clothes any other way.

[music out . . .]

Another BrandsFormation™!

Hangers' BrandsFormation™ is in the beginning stages, but already people are coming into Carl's stores and asking for the "dry cleaning geek."

Carl is dominating radio with his messages. He is committed to the long haul and to his BrandsFormation™.

Breaking it Down

- Bricks & Mortar is a process to simplify turning your Differentiating Idea into a strategy-based message.

- Bricks are always changing. They dramatize your point of difference.

- Bricks are cemented by the Mortar elements — *always*! Bricks are stories.

- Mortar is constant. These are the consistent elements that serve as cement between bricks.

Mortar elements: These never change.

- Music / color

- Voice / logo

- Words that differentiate. Words you want to "own."

www.brandsformation.com

Do you have the courage?

10

BrandsFormation™ Touchpoints

One of my BrandsFormation™ partners is the owner of a local chain of convenience stores in the Midwest. Valley Dairy has a lot going for it, including the owner, Monica Musich.

Monica is a smart, hard-working owner, involved in all aspects of the business. The Valley Dairy Stores have been in the Grand Forks area since the late 1950s. Monica fondly recalls growing up around the business which her father, Frank Schmidt, and his business associate, Norm Dufault, managed. She said it was great as a kid to be around a family business that sells candy and ice cream.

Convenience stores as a rule are high-traffic, low gas-margin businesses. Most people don't give much thought about their experiences in a convenience store. You go in, you get your milk or gas, you get out. Think about the convenience store you patronize. It's most likely a national chain, a clerk or two stand behind the register; maybe they speak to you, maybe not. They take your money and you're gone. I bet you couldn't pick the clerk (at your local store) out of a line-up of three people.

Still, the national stores keep stacking up, and Valley Dairy found itself in a situation that many small business owners find themselves: How are we going to compete and where do we begin?

To be sure, Valley Dairy was making it fine. They had more locations than anyone else, which is the position you want to hold in the "convenience" game, and it was a clear point of difference for them. They also had employees that had been with them for years. But even with a good business that has eight stores and four car washes, along with great employees, there were important issues to take care of before laying out their strategy and beginning their BrandsFormation™ campaign.

One of the important elements of my system is the Touchpoints Evaluation, and we conduct this with every client — no exceptions. We always find areas for improvement at this step and Valley Dairy was no exception. Included in our analysis, we noted that in several locations, the employees did not greet people as they walked in. In some locations we visited, we found the bathrooms were not as clean as they could be, which is critical for any retail establishment.

HOW TO FAIL FASTER

Let me pose and answer a question I briefly addressed earlier.

Can BrandsFormation™ help a failing business succeed? The answer is NO — BrandsFormation™ will help a failing business fail faster. It will *accelerate* your trip to Chapter 11.

Once again, BrandsFormation™ is about gaining and owning mindshare. It is about getting people *to think of you first* whenever they need your product or service, and having some sort of positive connection with you. However, there is no way for people to maintain "some sort of positive connection with you" if their experience of your product or service is negative.

Monica listened. She instituted a system for cleaning the restrooms on an hourly basis. She established bathroom cleanliness standards, and posted a check-list for their maintenance. Employees began greeting customers into the stores with a smile and saying "Hi" as they entered the door.

So, we set forth with our strategy. Valley Dairy had more locations, they were locally owned with long-time employees involved that lived in and are involved in the community. Our strategy-based message was apparent: "With more hometown locations than anyone else, you know wherever you go, you'll always hear: 'Welcome to Valley Dairy! Welcome Home!'"

Valley Dairy is another BrandsFormation™ success story. Like all good businesses, the owners had to take an honest look at themselves and now, they are "talking the talk and walking the walk."

THE COURAGE TO CHECK

How about you? Many business owners don't have the courage to really take a good hard look at themselves and their performance. Are you one of the few who will?

When you get right down to it, branding is about how to get someone into your store or try your service the first time. After that, it'll be up to you to perform if you want them to come back.

Applying the fundamentals of a successful business is how you build your brand. You only add marketing as the final step. Don't invite people until you are "at your best."

But if your business is bad or lacking for any reason, all the branding in the world won't help you, except to help you right out of business. Put lipstick on a pig, and it's still a pig. You can't advertise your way to superior performance. Performance is reality.

GIVING YOUR BUSINESS A CHECK UP
FROM THE NECK UP

This is why I spend valuable time conducting a Touchpoints Evaluation with each and every client. It is a structured method to evaluate every point of contact or interaction between something or someone from your company and a potential or current customer.

Sounds extensive, doesn't it? It is. The Touchpoints Evaluation is a tool to measure your business from poor to great in more than 40 different categories! Yes, it takes time, thought, effort — and courage! The rewards, however, are great for those who will.

One client wrote a report more than 20 pages long, with detailed paragraphs on every measure. You can be sure a small business owner who takes his business's

Touchpoints that seriously is going to build a great brand when he applies the BrandsFormation™ System.

Are you ready? Here it is. How does your business rate?

TOUCHPOINTS EVALUATION

There are five major headings:

- Marketing
- Consumer Perspective
- Price/Value
- Relationships
- Brand Platform

Beneath these are the 40+ specific areas to measure. Work through these, and you'll know how you are doing. And you'll know where you really need to go to work.

Marketing

	Poor–Great	
Strategy	1 2 3 4 5	NA
Frequency	1 2 3 4 5	NA
Consistency	1 2 3 4 5	NA
Emotional Connection	1 2 3 4 5	NA
Website	1 2 3 4 5	NA
Brochures	1 2 3 4 5	NA
Business Cards	1 2 3 4 5	NA
Signage	1 2 3 4 5	NA

Consumer Perspective

	Poor–Great	
Location	1 2 3 4 5	NA
Entryway	1 2 3 4 5	NA
Word of Mouth	1 2 3 4 5	NA
Community Involvement	1 2 3 4 5	NA
D.W.Y.S.Y.D.*	1 2 3 4 5	NA
Product Reliability	1 2 3 4 5	NA
WOW! Service	1 2 3 4 5	NA
Clean Bathrooms	1 2 3 4 5	NA
Business Vitality	1 2 3 4 5	NA
Convenient Hours	1 2 3 4 5	NA
Mindshare/Position	1 2 3 4 5	NA
Reputation/Image	1 2 3 4 5	NA
Parking	1 2 3 4 5	NA
Delivery	1 2 3 4 5	NA
Store Flow	1 2 3 4 5	NA
Customer Service	1 2 3 4 5	NA

*("Do what you say you do")

Price/Value

	Poor–Great	
Competitor's Pricing	1 2 3 4 5	NA
Communicated?	1 2 3 4 5	NA
Demonstrate Value	1 2 3 4 5	NA
Finance Options	1 2 3 4 5	NA
Benefits/Features	1 2 3 4 5	NA
Price or Cost?	1 2 3 4 5	NA
Quality Products	1 2 3 4 5	NA

Do you talk product/
service, or what the
product service does for
the customer?   1 2 3 4 5   NA

Relationships

	Poor–Great	
Connection with Client	1 2 3 4 5	NA
Predictability/Consistency	1 2 3 4 5	NA
Integrity	1 2 3 4 5	NA
Communicate Expertise	1 2 3 4 5	NA
Sacrifice	1 2 3 4 5	NA
Speed	1 2 3 4 5	NA
Welcoming Statement	1 2 3 4 5	NA
How Ya Doin'?	1 2 3 4 5	NA
Thanks	1 2 3 4 5	NA
Client's Name	1 2 3 4 5	NA

Brand Platform

Now take the three worst-rated areas you identified. Put some careful thinking time into answering. What is your game plan to improve?

How can we "WOW!" the customer at key Touchpoints?

How did you do? The most important thing now is, do you know where to go to work?

Breaking it Down

CHAPTER 10

- Do your business a favor and work through the Touchpoints Evaluation.

- Our firm conducts this analysis with every client — no exceptions.

- This tool will help you take a hard look at what you need to change about your business.

- Take the necessary steps to get your business in order before you start your BrandsFormation™ campaign.

www.brandsformation.com

Epilogue

YOUR LEGACY

I would like to conclude my book in the same way I close out my seminars, by reminding people that business is just a game. The real "P&L" that matters stands for People and Love — the people that you love, and how you honor those relationships.

I have been lucky in my life. Looking back I am struck by the incredible journey I've had to this point. Mine has been a life filled with love, laughter, sorrow, passion, drive, challenges, God, interesting experiences, and serious, but also fun work. As a young child growing up in the Midwest, I never once thought to myself, I want to work with businesses on strategy, and help to make a difference in their lives. Nope, I was more interested in girls, music and sailing. Yet, as it often happens, my life has turned out greater than the sum of my early dreams.

I am honored by the opportunities that have come my way. I have been surrounded by individuals and companies that are solid, forward-moving and principled. This has helped to shape me in countless ways. And, I understand that it's my responsibility to pass that on.

An unwavering principle that anchors both my personal and professional life is, *as long as you are doing things for the right reasons, and always with others in mind, things will fall into place.* It means something to me to help others, maybe it's my Boy Scouts training. I believe that no individual achievement can ever equal the fulfillment and the satisfaction of helping others to achieve their goals.

While my early ambitions did not include revolutionizing small businesses in America, it has become my dream and my passion, and I am going for it. No one ever got anywhere by sitting out, it's a pretty basic principle, but you have to get in the game if you ever expect a chance at winning. I made a choice to *get in the game*, and I'm in it to win!

The material things we spend time chasing — the sailboats, the cars, the money, the accolades — will all turn to rust and dust. You've heard it said, "you can't take it with you." Well, there is one thing you can take with you and that is what you leave behind … your legacy.

What will your legacy be? Are you living your life in a way that reflects your vision of your legacy? What will your children, and their children, and their children take from your life? What example will you give them to follow? Will the world they live in be a better place because of you?

You make the choice. You live the life. You create the legacy.

Endnotes

1. Jack Trout. Video-taped interview. Trout & Partners office. Old Greenwich, CT. November 19, 2003.

2. Alan M. Webber. "What Great Brands Do." *Fast Company.com.* Issue 10: August 1997.

3. Adapted from Jack Trout with Steve Rifkin. *Differentiate Or Die: Survival in Our Era of Killer Competition.* Hoboken, NJ: John Wiley & Sons, Inc. 2000, 6.

4. Jonathan Bond and Richard Kirshenbaum. *Under the Radar: Talking to Today's Cynical Consumer.* John Wiley & Sons, Inc., 1997., 15.

5. Webber. "What Great Brands Do."

6. Adapted from Jack Trout. *Trout on Strategy.* New York: McGraw-Hill, 2004, 14–29.

7. Al Ries and Jack Trout. *Positioning: The Battle for Your Mind.* New York: McGraw-Hill, 2001, 30.

8. Trout. Interview.

9. Trout. Strategy. 66.

10. *USA Today*, May 23, 2005, B3.

11. Al Ries and Laura Ries. *The 22 Immutable Laws of Branding.* Harper Collins, 1998, 19.